T0266961

FLYING FORTRESS GUNNER

FLYING FORTRESS GUNNER

B-17 BALL TURRET GUNNER BOB HARPER'S 35 COMBAT MISSIONS OVER GERMANY

OTHER SCHIFFER BOOKS ON RELATED SUBJECTS

Serenade to the Big Bird: A New Edition of the Classic B-17 Tribute,
Bert Stiles, 978-0-7643-1396-7

The Clay Pigeons: A B-17 Pilot's Story of World War II,
E. Helene Sage, 978-0-7643-3951-6

Library of Congress Control Number: 2023931139

Designed by Christopher Bower
Cover design by Christopher Bower
Type set in Abolition/Baskerville

ISBN: 978-0-7643-6706-9
Printed in China

Published by Schiffer Publishing, Ltd.
4880 Lower Valley Road
Atglen, PA 19310
Phone: (610) 593-1777; Fax: (610) 593-2002
Email: Info@schifferbooks.com
Web: www.schifferbooks.com

For our complete selection of fine books on this and related subjects, please visit our website at www.schifferbooks.com. You may also write for a free catalog.

Schiffer Publishing's titles are available at special discounts for bulk purchases for sales promotions or premiums. Special editions, including personalized covers, corporate imprints, and excerpts, can be created in large quantities for special needs. For more information, contact the publisher.

We are always looking for people to write books on new and related subjects. If you have an idea for a book, please contact us at proposals@schifferbooks.com.

CONTENTS

INTRODUCTION: WHY SOME STORIES NEED TO BE TOLD

Before beginning Bob's adventures as a belly-turret gunner with the 381st Bombardment Group (BG), I thought I would take a moment to explain how I met Bob and came to write his story and why writers might feel the need to keep telling "new" stories of an "old" war that ended over seventy-five years ago. Of course, feel free to skip right ahead to chapter 1, where Bob's story begins, when both he and the Barling Bomber arrive in St. Louis, Missouri, in the year 1923. Or continue here and meet up with two contemporaries of Bob; a Nazi Luftwaffe pilot and a political prisoner who spent six years in a Nazi concentration camp. They have a lot to do with why I wrote this book.

When I was a boy growing up on Long Island in the 1950s, I watched my share of war movies on our black-and-white television set, most of them starring John Wayne. Though my father and four uncles had served in the Army and Navy during World War II, they never talked about the war in front of us kids. Still, a few stories began to trickle out from other men who had been in combat. When I was ten years old, Jack, who lived with his grandfather in the house next to my grandparents, showed us his war trophies and let me hold a short samurai sword. Jack was a US Marine, still suffering from PTSD, who had fought in the Pacific campaign and had the scars and medals to show for it. Then there was Mr. Levine, a neighbor and officer in the merchant marine whose ship had survived an attack by a German U-boat wolf pack, on the "Murmansk Run." Mr. Razler, my tenth-grade history teacher, an Army Ranger training for the assault on the Japanese home islands, spent an entire class talking about his time preparing for the invasion. "They told us to be sure to write our final letters home; it was going to be bad for those of us in the first wave, up to 95 percent casualties. But I was saved from that fate when we dropped the bomb on Hiroshima." Those stories and more were told reluctantly, with little opportunity for questions, almost as if these men were blurting out their tales by mistake, then realizing that they really didn't want to talk about those days after all.

Then in 1971 I had my first run-in with the enemy, an ex-Luftwaffe pilot who lived across the street from my parents. Fritz was the friendliest man on the block, known for his booming laugh that you could hear six houses away. "He's harmless," my mom told me in way of explanation. "He had a bad time during the war, so he laughs a lot now."

But there was more to Fritz's story, and he shared it with me one night. I was home from college and serving as the volunteer bartender at my parent's Fourth of July barbecue, and Fritz was a frequent visitor to that makeshift bar. We struck up a conversation; he was impressed that I was in college, and confided in me that going to college had also been his dream. I asked him what had happened.

"The war happened . . . I began with the German Boy Scouts, you know? When I was just in short pants, a young boy. Everyone joined. Then going from there to Hitler Youth was what was expected of you. It was like a big club; we camped and played in the woods. Learned to box and did some target shooting. . . . They kept us busy, but we had a good time too. . . . Then I joined a youth flying club; maybe I was fifteen or sixteen. So, you go from one thing to the next and suddenly you are in the Luftwaffe." He let go an innocent laugh. "Only nineteen years old and I was a Stuka pilot!"

I was fascinated and asked a lot of questions, egging him on. For a fledgling writer this was good material, more so because it was coming from the enemy's perspective. So, Fritz told me about his first days leading up to combat, the sense of freedom that an airplane gave him, high above the earth. Then he told me about getting captured. After three months in North Africa, he was shot down but parachuted to safety behind German lines. Then, just a month later, he was shot down a second time. "My plane was smoking, and I headed out over the sea. But it was no use . . . so, I parachuted out, but I got tangled up in my parachute when I hit the water. I swallowed a lot of salt water and started vomiting. . . . I was drowning, the waves dragging me down. . . . A British patrol boat came to the rescue; they cut me out of the parachute harness, hauled me out of the sea, saved my life."

Then Fritz told me that he had spent over three years in POW camps. "I learned English, so there was that. But it was pretty bad. Not worth talking about. . . . I never want to see another turnip again!" he summed it up with his crazy laugh.

"Yeah, the war was sad," I said. "I've read about it . . . it ruined a lot of lives."

For some reason, that brought Fritz around to Germany's defeat. "The war was terrible," he conceded, probably thinking back to his ravaged homeland. "But none of it was Germany's fault," this newly minted American suddenly claimed, an angry tone entering his voice. "We were betrayed by them . . . they tricked us into war," Fritz stated drunkenly, repeating the Nazi propaganda, and pointing over the fence to our neighbor's yard, our Jewish neighbor's yard. "It was their fault, the Jews, die Juden," he muttered, angrily. I immediately told him how ridiculous that was.

....

"No. No." He lowered his voice, still friendly, then grabbed my shoulder and pointed again at the fence. "It was the Jews. The Jewish bankers . . . they were behind the whole thing."

He stood there for a moment before realizing his mistake. Then he walked away without another word, shaking his head and laughing that crazy laugh. Soon after, he said his goodbyes. The next day, I told my parents what had transpired. After that, they steered clear of the man the best they could.

A few years after I discovered this unrepentant Nazi living in my neighborhood, I met one of the many millions of victims of the Nazi war machine. It was 1975, and I was living and working in Manhattan, studying German at night in a classroom high up in the World Trade Center, determined to finally gain fluency in a second language (I never did). Twice a week, I would head over after work, just a short walk from Wall Street, and enter the massive lobby of the North Tower. Then I'd take the express elevator, a little like riding the New York's subway system (but much cleaner), get off at one of the sky lobbies, and then take a local elevator up to my floor. Those tall towers were built with elasticity in mind and, when a strong wind blew, could sway up to 3 feet. You could actually feel it moving! But the swaying classroom also served as a great icebreaker for the ten of us adults sitting there nervously that first week. Chatting before class, we soon became friends and a few weeks later decided to get together to share a drink at a nearby café.

Though we invited our old professor Frau G. to come along with us, she declined. There was a seriousness about her, a German formality from a different age, that we couldn't pierce. Well, with one exception. It was our last class of the semester, and Christmas was just around the corner. "I want to share a story with you tonight," she said as she began the class, and then handed each of us a single sheet, photocopied on both sides. "I'll read it out loud to you first in German." She began, "*Die Kleinen Pferde*." Though I was the worst student in the class, even I could translate that much: *The Little Horses*.

Five minutes later she was done, and the class was quiet. Though most of us didn't have the vocabulary yet for such a story, I think we all got the drift; *Die Kleinen Pferde* was about a German prison camp.

"I know that might have been too difficult to translate on first pass, but your final class project is to do just that," she said. "Before you go tonight, I will give each of you a stamped letter with my address on it. You won't get your final grade until I get that translation back. But I also want to give you some background on that story first, and how it came to be. I'm sure it will motivate you to do a good job."

"In the 1930s," she continued in her clear, but heavily accented English:

My husband, Hans, and I were both professors at a university in Germany. I left my job when I became pregnant with our first child, and Hans continued teaching. Teaching government and law, very dangerous subjects at the time in Germany. Soon Hans was getting a lot of pressure to change the content of the courses, but he resisted. One day an old friend told us that he had heard Hans was going to be fired, arrested, and relocated, in that order. Whatever Hans had said in a classroom about Hitler and those thugs, he had finally gone too far. But thanks to this tip, we managed to escape to Switzerland, where Hans had some family. Still, we left behind most everything. . . . You can't imagine how little of your life can fit in two suitcases.

Our closest friends, another young couple much like us, stayed on at the university. Bettina taught art, and her husband, Friedrich, was in the Government Studies Department with my husband. Though Friedrich tried to tone it down, he was an antifascist to his very core, and therefore under close surveillance by the Nazi secret police. Like a lot of people, Bettina and Friedrich thought they had time. That something would happen to the little tyrant, and all would be well again. So, they stayed put. But the next year, Germany invaded Poland and the real war began. Soon after, they were arrested and sent to a special prison for Germans, a camp for political enemies of the state. For the first few months it wasn't too bad. Then Bettina and their six-year-old daughter were separated from Friedrich when he was sent to a construction camp. *Sklavenarbeitslager.* Slave labor camp. And all contact between them was cut off.

After a couple of years in the camp there was very little to eat for Bettina and her child, and little coal or wood for the stove in their hut. As winter came on, they slept huddled together in their threadbare jackets and hats, trying to stay warm. Somehow, though, Bettina managed to fashion a little horse for her daughter to play with, a wire-and-metal sculpture. It was meant to be a surprise Christmas present for the girl, so she kept it carefully hidden away. But on one particularly bad day three weeks before Christmas, she decided that her daughter needed something to cheer her up, so she gave the girl the little horse. *Das kleine Pferd.*

A few days later, Bettina heard her number called on the camp speakers: *Zum Wachhaus, schnell! To the guardhouse, quickly!* That was never something that you wanted to hear. She looked for her daughter, who had been playing with friends, but couldn't find her. In a panic she rushed to the guardhouse, thinking something had happened to the little girl.

Inside it was so warm, she told me, that in her half-starved condition she almost passed out. They pushed her into a room where her daughter was seated in a chair, the little horse on the table in front of her.

"Where did you get the material to make that horse?" the sergeant barked at her.

"Just a bit of wire and metal that I found," she gestured out at the camp. "I swear I didn't steal anything. It's just a toy for my child," she pleaded, expecting blows to follow.

The senior guard gave her a strange look, almost of embarrassment. "Well, Christmas is coming," he said gruffly. "Do you think you can make more of these?"

So that same day, Bettina began making toys in a little room in the back of the camp, with only her daughter for company. It was warm in there, and the food was enough to keep them alive. The guards supplied her with paint, wood, wire, cloth, and metal scraps. She turned them into beautiful gifts for their children's birthdays and, of course, presents for each Christmas season. As the war began to go badly for the Germans, there were fewer and fewer goods to buy in the stores, and her value as a toymaker increased even more. After the war, Bettina reunited with her husband, who had somehow survived the six years as well. Later the three of them came and visited us in Switzerland. . . . So, you see? A happy ending."

We sat there in complete silence. The woman sitting next to me, who worked days at a German freight company, wiped away a tear.

"I know that you did not expect this to be part of your lesson tonight," she continued in a soft voice. "But if we don't share stories like these, the world will forget what happened. Besides"—the old woman smiled a tired smile—"can you imagine a better Christmas story?"

Ten years after my job in New York ended, I made acquaintance with B-17 gunner Bob Harper. I was at a wedding reception being held under an expansive, yellow-striped tent in upstate New York. A short man, looking very dapper in a tuxedo, approached me, and we renewed the introductions that had been made earlier at the church. Bob's son had just married my wife's sister, and you couldn't have imagined a happier man that day. It quickly turned out that Bob had already heard about our mountainside homestead in Vermont, and he wanted to know more about our life up there, living in a cabin, cooking, and heating with wood. So, I picked out an adventure that had happened just the previous month, when my wife ran into a big black bear while pushing the baby stroller on our deserted dirt road. It was a good story. But as often happens at wedding receptions, we were soon interrupted. As we shook hands farewell, he promised to visit us in Vermont someday. Ten years later, Bob and his wife, Katy, did just that, and we talked about a lot of things that afternoon in our kitchen, including our shared interest in woodworking. But still nothing about Bob's time during the war.

Our baby boy who was in the stroller the "day of the bear" eventually grew up and attended Washington University in Bob's hometown of St. Louis. During a visit to our son's campus, Bob and Katy took all of us out to dinner. I told Bob that I was working on my first novel. Bob mentioned that he had recently written an account of his time spent as a belly-turret gunner on a B-17 with the 381st Bomb Group out of Ridgewell, England. When I returned to Vermont, a copy of his journal was waiting for me in the mail. It was brief, only fifteen pages or so, but included a detailed description of what life was like as a B-17 belly gunner, flying thirty-five combat missions with the 533rd Squadron. When I ran into Bob a year later, I mentioned that I thought there was a good story there and that he should try to get it into print.

Another decade passed. We were moving to a new house when I found Bob's journal in a forgotten corner of one of our many bookshelves where I kept my "writing projects for another day." It was sitting right on top of Frau G.'s faded photocopy of *Der Kleinen Pferden*. I sat there in the empty room rereading them. Then I gave Bob a call and asked him if he had any photos from his time with the 381st BG. His son emailed me some great ones. I was starting to think that maybe we had enough for a magazine article. Just as I began an outline, things took a fortuitous turn and I connected with the 381st BG Memorial Group on Facebook.

With the help of Chris Tennet of the memorial group, I came up with Bob's complete mission list along with the names, numbers, and crew lists of all fourteen B-17s that Bob had flown on. The memorial group also gave me access to the combat diaries of the 533rd Squadron, the 381st

Bomb Group, and the 242nd Medical Detachment. Not long after that, the Harper family provided me with a wonderful collection of letters that Bob sent home during the war, along with more photos of his crew and planes. Finally, I managed to interview Robert Pearce, the nephew of Lt. Joe Pearce, Bob's pilot, who generously lent me his own research on his uncle's time with the 381st BG. It felt like there was way too much to condense into a magazine article; it had to be a book.

I began interviewing Bob by phone with specific questions and filled two notebooks, spending some very enjoyable hours talking to him about his recollections of those days. Some of the details that he shared were about the actual combat, but mostly it was what it was like to be a young American, before, during, and after the war. Then during COVID, with the world in lockdown, I finally started writing "Bob's Book," as we called it. In his late nineties then, and living in an assisted-care home, Bob told me that he felt that surviving COVID was his thirty-sixth combat mission. I replied, "Waiting for me to finally finish writing your story, Bob, will probably be your thirty-seventh."

It has been a great experience and honor to work with Bob Harper, one of the many brave men who risked their lives when they took to the skies to fight the Nazis. Bob remained incredibly humble throughout this process, telling me more than once that "I am not a hero, Bill. We had a job to do, and we did it; some days it was much harder than others."

During World War II, 135,000 airmen served with the 8th Army Air Force, flying over three million individual missions. Twenty-eight thousand of these airmen were killed in action, more than all the losses that US Marines suffered during the entire war (19,733). This is the story of one of those 135,000 airmen: his journey to the war and his long journey home, earned one combat mission at a time.

If we don't share stories like these, the world will forget what happened.

Bill Cullen

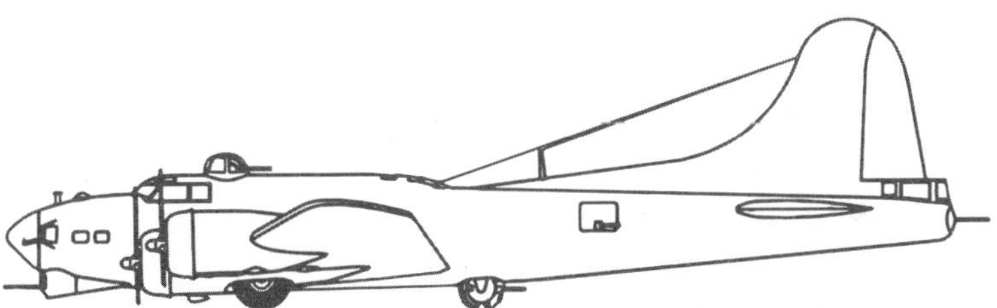

CHAPTER 1
ON THE WAY TO WAR

When Bob Harper was born in St. Louis, Missouri, in April 1923, the second son to Eva and Joseph Harper, the world was at peace. World War I had ended five years prior, and the Great Depression was still six years in the future. Bob's father, Joseph, was a young dentist, and his wife, Eva, an avid gardener known for her lovely rose beds. The Harpers lived in a large, three-story brick house in a peaceful tree-lined neighborhood just a block from the St. Louis Botanical Garden.

Like most Americans in 1923, the Harpers were enjoying the newfound optimism surging through postwar America, fueled in part by almost daily discoveries and breakthroughs in science, technology, and medicine. Agricultural innovations now promised plentiful food for the world. Powered by an ever-expanding supply of electricity, *newfangled* inventions were increasing productivity in workplaces and decreasing drudgery in the home. That summer, when St. Louis hosted the world's largest air show, every innovation in the world of aviation arrived along with it.

One of the biggest draws of the air show was the US Army's Barling Bomber. Only twenty years prior, the Wright Brothers had made their fledgling flight in the Wright Flyer, a frail 600-pound biplane with a wingspan of 40 feet, powered by a single 12 hp gasoline motor. Now, just two decades later, thousands of spectators would view the 28-foot-tall Barling Bomber, marvel at its 120-foot wingspan, and feel the power of the six 420 hp, liquid-cooled engines thundering noisily through the fairgrounds. The new bomber was a prototype designed to protect American shores by intercepting hostile fleets while they were still 200 miles out to sea. High-speed fighter biplanes, new parachute designs, and machine guns were also on display, along with a tent full of new and more-accurate bombs. The world may have been at peace in 1923, but it was clear that the many military leaders who attended the show were already planning for the next one.

After a week, the air show was over, the tents were taken down, and the 374 participating airplanes dispersed back to their home fields across America. Life in St. Louis went back to normal, and that is where we meet young Bob Harper, attending public schools, playing in his neighborhood, and enjoying a happy childhood, even when it was overtaken by arrival of the

Great Depression in 1929. Like most kids growing up back then, Bob told me that he and his friends needed few props or toys, especially with the nearby 80-acre Shaw's Botanical Gardens for a playground:

> Everyone that worked in those beautiful gardens knew our gang, and we had the run of the place. Right next to the gardens was the city's 280-acre Tower Grove Park, where I learned to play both tennis and golf at an early age. That came in handy later, because I made the high school tennis team and got to compete alongside some of the best young talent in the St. Louis area. I remember this time in my life as being pretty well perfect, and I guess I thought that college might be next. . . . There was no rush; back then it felt like I had all the time in the world to figure things out.

But by the time that Bob graduated from Roosevelt High School in June 1941, war was a loud drumbeat in the background. The previous month, the Germans had taken the island of Crete in a massive airborne attack, depriving England of an important base in the Mediterranean. This was followed by the Germans executing an even bolder move with the initiation of Operation Barbarossa, invading Russia with 140 divisions and destroying most of Russia's air force (1,200 planes) by noon of the first day. The Germans seemed unstoppable. In Asia, Japan's armed forces were about to take complete control of French Indochina, and their intentions to rule their part of the world were clearer than ever.

As Roosevelt's Class of '41 headed out into the world that summer, some going on to college, others looking for a job, America was headed down the path to war. Though most Americans suspected that the peace wouldn't last, none of Bob's high school friends imagined that in the coming four years, over one hundred graduates of Roosevelt High School would die in the service of their country. Then suddenly America *was* in the war. I spoke to Bob about this time of his life.

"Did you think about volunteering after Pearl Harbor?" I asked in my first interview:

> No, it really didn't cross my mind. Or, at least, not seriously. I had just gotten out of high school. I was eighteen years old and a little over 5 feet, 4 inches tall and about 110 pounds, which didn't even meet the Army's minimum requirements at that time. Though I was in great shape from playing tennis and lifting weights, I didn't

have the physical stature that you associate with warriors running off and volunteering to go to war. Like you see in the movies [Bob paused and chuckled]. I had just started a job with Anheuser-Busch. Though it wasn't an interesting one, just a purchasing clerk in the brewery department, yeast and other supplies, still it felt good. Remember, I grew up in the Great Depression, men standing on lines looking for work . . . and for food for their families. So even though jobs were growing much more plentiful, to have steady work at eighteen was really something.

So, I worked at Anheuser-Busch for a year or so. Toward the end of '42, I got lucky and landed a good job out at Parks Air College, just across the river in Cahokia. They were training pilots there, using PT-19 two-seater monoplanes, which were fabricated from metal and wood. I had enjoyed my high school woodshop courses, got good marks, and I guess that counted for something, because I got that job at the base right off, working in the PT-19 maintenance sheds. Boy, I loved fixing those planes. I was content to do my part in the war effort while staying in the background! And the position came along with a Class 2A, Occupational Deferment. So that put off any decisions on enrollment.

Bob laughed, remembering back:

You know, Parks Air College was a busy place to work. You got a sense of urgency back then; they were training so many pilots all at once, and we all had a sense of purpose keeping those trainers going, like we were an important part of the war effort. We all suspected that we would be called up, but most guys were not in a big rush to get going. When things settled down a little after Pearl Harbor, it felt like it was going to be a long, long war. . . . We'd all get our chance. That's what everyone was saying . . . and turns out they were right!

In December 1942, President Roosevelt ended all volunteer enlistments to protect the home-front labor pool, which was constantly depleted in an unorganized manner when well-trained men left their jobs to volunteer, often walking away from important occupations in vital war industries to join up with one branch of the armed services or another. In theory, the new, all-encompassing draft would selectively build out the armed services and, through intense screening, figure out who was best qualified for any given branch, filling in gaps in the personnel as needed. Though Bob was doing an important job out at Parks Air College, his Class 2-A was soon revoked:

> My perfect job repairing PT-19s came to an end along with my idea of going off to college someday. I loved working on those planes; it was a great bunch of guys out at Parks, and I was learning a lot. But by mid-1943, the war was raging on two fronts, and frankly they needed bodies to fight it. And lots of them. Much to my dismay, they pulled my deferment. Ah, my happy life at Parks was over. But I understood.
>
> So, when I was drafted into the service in April 1943, I didn't hesitate to answer the call. I reported right on schedule to the Jefferson Barracks in St. Louis later that summer, just miles from my parents' house, and that's where it all started. Suddenly I was on my way to war, and I really had no idea how many stops I would make along the way.

Bob recorded his recollections of those first days in a journal written years after the war. It offers a great insight into just what a young recruit faced in Army basic training in the summer of 1943:

> You were supposed to be at least 5 feet, 5 inches tall and 125 pounds, but at the time I was just a little over 5 feet, 4 inches and 110 pounds. But they listed me at 5 feet, 5 inches, and I guess they figured if they could add an inch to my height, well, they could fatten me up as well and add those necessary fifteen pounds, so they just wrote down 125 pounds, and it became a fact. When they took me, I was sure that I'd be the shortest man in the US Army.
>
> But I was also very physically fit at the time. I did a lot of weightlifting back then. I had also played tennis on the Roosevelt High team and kept it up after I graduated, playing after work and whenever I had the chance. So, after a physical exam, which I passed with flying colors, and then getting three or four shots in the same arm, one right after the other (welcome to the Army), they sent me through a supply line to get my clothes. The quartermaster was so happy to see me and said, "I've had this pair of 5-D shoes in stock so long that I'm sure glad to see you and get rid of 'em!"

Nothing else fit me; not even close. My pants and shirt sleeves were about six inches too long. Mom and Dad came down to the barracks that night, and bless her, Mom took them home and shortened them and Dad got them back to me the next morning. . . . So at least I looked halfway presentable. Then the Army gave me a haircut and I looked like a shaved chicken. So much for looking presentable.

After two weeks at the Jefferson Barracks, they sent us by train to Lincoln, Nebraska, for basic training. It was a long ride to get there, about 450 miles or so, with lots of local stops. The train was jammed with raw recruits from all walks of life. In such close quarters we quickly got to know each other, sharing a little of our backgrounds, families, etc. In my group were college professors, laborers, and everything in between, aged from eighteen to thirty-seven (the top age). When we got to the Lincoln Army Base, it became more organized as they sorted us out, sixty-four to a barracks. I was in an upper bunk, and my meager belongings were stored in a barracks bag at the foot of our bunk.

Our barracks had a short old army sergeant, and he was tough! Sergeant Reinboldt was his name, and he tried to get us in shape and teach us a little respect for all ranks above our status of buck privates. He'd come into our barracks about dawn every morning and scream, "In sixty seconds I want you guys in front of the barracks like four rows of corn!" That would set off organized chaos, a race to get dressed and out there for roll call with the sun still low on the horizon. Then we'd go to breakfast, where we'd line up with our aluminum trays and the cooks would more or less throw the food at us. Although it seemed to be popular to complain about the army food, for some reason I always did enjoy it. So basic training was a great experience, a great mixture of all kinds of personalities and people. But you learned to get along. It was intense but they wanted to get us fit for whatever assignment we had coming.

Some of us had a harder time than others. Our old butcher from the 39th Street market named Eckert was in my group. He had a terrible time with our physical training because it was tough, and he was overweight and thirty-five years old to boot. We'd climb ropes, take long, long hikes with heavy backpacks, and do all types of calisthenics. This put us in good physical shape.

In our barracks was an old golf pro named Leland Gibson from Kansas City; we called him the Duke. The Duke was also thirty-five years old, but as an athlete, in much-better shape than the other older recruits. After the war, he continued to play professional golf, appearing in sixteen US Opens and ten Masters Championships, and won the PGA Quarter-Century Championship, even hitting a hole-in-one at the 1957 Masters. Gibson was just one example of the thousands of fine athletes, entertainers, and movie stars that put their careers on hold to serve their country in World War II. Like I said, we were all in it together, men from different walks of life, for sure.

Unfortunately for me, one of the first exercises was boxing—some afternoons we boxed for 3 hours. I'm not kidding! We really had a tough physical training instructor, and he believed in hardening us up for what was coming. We used 16-ounce gloves, and Gad, were they heavy after swinging them for several hours! He started us from scratch, showing us the proper footwork. Guard, jabs, defense, etc. Then he paired us off and we fought two-minute rounds. There were only several other recruits even close to my size, and this tough little Italian kid from Brooklyn named Tony wound up as my partner most days. . . . He beat me up regularly. I was a terrible boxer, but we had a lot of practice and eventually I managed to limit Tony's damage!

From his induction into the Army until his final discharge over two years later, Bob would do his best to keep his family up to date on his progress through both training and combat, though often leaving the grimmer details for another time. His first letter home was from boot camp and gives a rare firsthand account of a young recruit training up in the frozen North, with no idea of where the war would take him but intent on keeping his sense of humor and a positive outlook.

Lincoln, Nebraska
August 12, 1943

Dear Folks,
Today was my first real day of hard, hard work. We were up at 5:30 as usual, and was it cold! (35 degrees) burrrr. You have to fall out in the cold, make your bed, and fall in formation at 5:45. I've never been so cold in my life, but we're sure learning to take it and like it. We have no choice!

At 6:30 we GI the barracks (scrub it). At 7:00 we fell out and went to the drill field for three hours with two ten-minute breaks. Close drilling consisted of all the flank movements (everyone moves at once, together, right or left face, to the rear march, extend march; to the half right march, etc.). I'm getting good—unconsciously—after so much pounding it comes natural.

We were then marched to the obstacle course, where we took a physical fitness exam. It consisted of a 300-yard dash, timed, pull-ups, push-ups, etc. The number of times you do things correctly are judged by the corporals. I hope you don't think I'm bragging, but I was ranked 4th in my whole flight (64 men). After basic training is over, we will take the test again, and my improvement will be recorded on my Army classification card, so it might help some time or other—you can never tell. This card follows you throughout your whole army life. It has your IQ, test grades, etc.

We had chow at 12:00, and then I went to the PX to get some menthol ChapStick. At 1:00 we had a clothing issue. I got all my buttons and air corps badges. I also got a pair of fatigues, four sizes too large. I guess I will just have to wait for them to get in some smaller sizes.

At 2:00 p.m. we had close-order rifle drill. Yep! I put a rifle on my shoulder for the first time. Man! It is heavy! Nine and a half pounds! We drilled for three and a half hours. I did fine and like it a lot.

After my shower I feel wonderful. I'm not a bit tired but tremendously hungry! Chow is in a few minutes!

My physical test today sure made me feel good that I did so well.

So, Patsy thinks that I will have a hard time? Well maybe she is right, but I will be in the ditch with the rest of them if the going gets too bad.

Oh yes, I was issued my gas mask today along with my canteen. We carry it all day, from 5:45 to 5:00—all the time—they really weigh.

Well, that's all for now. Write if anything new happens.

Love, Bob

The next stop for Bob was gunnery school in Las Vegas, Nevada, where he would train on one of Americas giant bombers, the B-17 Flying Fortress. Powered by four turbocharged Wright R-1820 Cyclone engines, the B-17G could fly fully loaded over Mt. Everest, at 29,000 feet the highest mountain in the world. The journey from a 1903 Wright flyer that could barely get off the ground, to the giant 1923 Barling Bomber that couldn't clear the Appalachians, to the 1943 version of the model B-17G had taken only forty years. Soon Bob would learn how to operate the Browning AN/M2 .50-caliber machine gun to defend his B-17G from German fighters, and if things went wrong, how to survive in the frozen skies, 5 miles above the earth.

CHAPTER 2
THE BALL TURRET

Never forget that a caliber .50 machine gun is essentially a terrific explosion wrapped up in a metal package. When the gun is handled properly, it controls that explosion so that nobody can be hurt but the enemy. But one instant of carelessness may release that packaged power at the wrong time, or in the wrong direction. Never let that happen to you. Make these safety rules your safety bible.
—Army Air Force manual "This is Your Gun," 1943

When Bob finished basic training in Lincoln, he was sent to gunnery school in Las Vegas, New Mexico. An interview with Bob in 2018, along with his journal and letters written when he first arrived in England, tells the story of an airman undergoing an extensive period of training for war:

> Towards the end of my stay at Lincoln Army Base they gave us an Army Air Force 64 physical, which was the toughest Air Force physical they had. I don't know why I passed, but I did, and they assigned me to aerial gunnery school at Las Vegas Air Force Base. The next day I was on a train to Nevada to become an aerial gunner.
>
> I was in a state of shock because I wanted to go to one of the advanced Army schools at Lincoln to get some college training. But there was no chance because the war was escalating so fast. Like most things in Army life, we had to grin and bear it . . . or at least bear it. So, three days later we arrived in Las Vegas after another long train ride, over 1,200 miles, start and stop. Once again, they put us in a barracks, and it was a new group with lots of new faces.
>
> We began training by shooting skeet on a skeet range every day. Those 12-gauge shotguns had quite a kick; my shoulder sure got black and blue. Then we'd have target practice with rifles. Most importantly, they taught us to lead the targets as they moved. I had never fired anything before, except a little .22-caliber target pistol when I was a boy, and only a few times at that. It quickly turned out though that I was a pretty good shot . . . I think my eye and hand coordination developed from so many hours of competitive tennis might have had something to do with it. I certainly had no firearms background.

Next up was learning to shoot the .50-caliber Browning AN/M2 machine guns, which we did at first on the ground for several weeks. Because of my size, being so short, they immediately assigned me to train as a ball turret gunner. They gave us a 90-page operational manual on the machine gun to study, and of course we learned to field-strip it blind, as well as detail-strip it down to its 300 parts back in the shop. Clean it. Learn everything about its automatic guidance sight.

During the 1930s, the US Army had come up with two versions of their "giant bomber." One of them, Boeing's B-17, was dubbed the "Flying Fortress" by a newspaper reporter who was impressed with its array of twelve .50-caliber machine guns. Each B-17 included a permanently affixed, defensive ball turret on its bottom side equipped with two AN/M2 .50 machine guns. The ball turret protected the belly of the B-17 from enemy fighters rising in attack from below or coming in from behind, while also offering a second opportunity to take a shot at fighters diving through the formation from above. Barely 4 feet across on the outside, it was designed to create minimum drag on the big plane and was usually staffed with the smallest gunner on the crew.

The ball turret's equipment and controls were innovative and compact. The left foot controlled the "reflector sight range reticule." The right foot operated a push-to-talk intercom switch. The turret could be pointed in any direction, starting with straight down, then up to the underside of the plane, and finally could be spun a full 360 degrees. Its directional control consisted of the two handgrips that also had firing buttons for the twin .50 machine guns. After the B-17 reached 10,000 feet or so and found its place in the bombing formation, its belly-turret gunner would enter from his position waiting in the fuselage. Closing the door behind him, he would rotate the ball turret into position. Then he would hook up to the oxygen and plug into the electric circuit to power up his heated flying suit and finally hook up to the bomber's intercom.

In combat, bombers and high-speed fighters would often engage each other at combined speeds of well over 500 mph. To help the turret gunners track these fighters, the ball turret was equipped with an automatic gunsight. Here is how a *Life* magazine article (January 24, 1944) explained it to the American public:

> One of the newer Sperry gadgets is the automatic gunsight, which is used in US bomber gun turrets. The gunner lines up his target with two vertical hairlines in the sight. The trick is to keep the enemy plane

> exactly framed in these lines, which are moved in or out by means of a range knob as the target approaches or recedes. As he follows the target in its course, the sight automatically makes deductions from this "tracking" process, which translates into the relative course and speed of the target. Taking this data, the range data, and other factors like the weight of the .50-caliber bullets, the gears and levers and circuits that make up the mechanical brain arrive with inhuman speed at an answer. The answer is expressed at the critical moment when the gunner presses his triggers and fires his .50-caliber machine guns at a target. The gunner's accuracy is not 100 percent. But is far higher than it has ever been before in the short-lived history of combat aviation.

As innovative as the Sperry gunsight was for accuracy, the two Browning AN/M2 .50-caliber machine guns that it was guiding were just as remarkable. Modified and still in use today almost eighty years later, the M2 machine gun could fire six hundred to eight hundred rounds a minute down its rifled barrels. At the heart of the M2's deadly effectiveness and power were its bullets. Designed with a tapered end that reduced drag and increased stability, it was large enough for a hollow center that could be packed with tracer or incendiary cores. The M2's accuracy and power made it the weapon of choice both on US bombers and fighter planes. During World War II, the 8th AF's big bombers would fire a staggering forty-four million .50 rounds in 1944 alone:

> So perfect is the shape of the ball (bullet), in fact, that a generation later, when engineers at Bell Aircraft were deciding on the shape for the X-1 supersonic research aircraft that would break Mach 1, they based it on the .50-caliber round of the M2. . . . Even today, ordnance engineers look in awe and wonder at the vision and genius of the .50-caliber round, designed at a time when slide rules, adding machines, and blackboards were the high-tech tools of the gun making trade. (John Gresham, *Warfare History* magazine)

According to Bob Harper, operating that innovative ball turret with its powerful twin 50s was a skill that took many weeks of training to hone. Eventually his every move became instinctive, and he was able to just focus on framing the target in the Sperry gunsight while he tuned out everything else that was going on elsewhere in his bomber. In a series of interviews, Bob recounted his long journey through gunnery and crew-training schools on his way to the war:

Being the smallest guy in my barracks at gunnery school, it came as no surprise to me when they told me I needed to get familiar with the ball turret, though eventually I also did some training on the waist guns and tail gun position. One morning, our gunnery officer gave us the word, "Your guns aren't doing any damn good down here; time to get 'em up in the air!"

So off we went, into the wild blue yonder. . . . We take flying for granted now; it is part of our way of life. But you have to understand that back in 1943, most civilians had never been in an airplane. I certainly hadn't. So, my first flight was a little shocking. We climbed on board this incredibly noisy, vibrating giant; a B-17 bomber. I took a seat on a bench that they had set up there for us gunners to wait our turns at the guns. I don't even think that the bench was attached to anything, so we just held on to a strap that was bolted to the wall . . .

I will never forget that first time I ever climbed down into a ball turret; they closed the lid on me and I rotated into position. We were probably only 5,000 or 6,000 feet up, so we didn't have the heavy flying suits on that we would wear later when we were practicing at higher altitudes. Suddenly I was down there all by myself in that turret and petrified. During that first flight we hit an air pocket while I was taking my turn, and the B-17 dropped 200 or 300 feet, and I thought the ball turret had fallen out of the airplane! I was scared to death. But after continued flights, my position became comfortable, and I actually grew to like it down there in the ball turret.

For our aerial gunnery training, another plane would tow a big trailing white sock, and we'd all be assigned to shoot at this sock. They were training all the gunners on the plane. We had a tail gunner, two waist gunners, a ball turret gunner, the radio operator had a gun sticking out of the top of the plane, the engineer-top turret gunner had two .50-caliber guns, the navigator and the bombardier each had a gun in their possession, plus a chin turret with two fifties. In all, we had twelve .50 calibers on the plane. I guess that's why they called our plane a flying fortress; there was a machine gun aiming in every direction.

I remember on my first flight when I swung my guns around, I could see the four propellers and I thought I might shoot one of the props off. I quickly learned that they had a cam that shut my guns off if they pointed at any of the propellers; that kept you from making a fatal mistake.

My guns were right next to my knees, and I'd look through my legs and out through a round glass about 2 feet in diameter. To rotate the turret, I would reach over my head, where there were two handles. Turning the handles in any direction would actuate the turret in the same direction. The triggers for my two .50s were on top of the handles. Directly in front of me was an electronic gunsight. You could frame an enemy fighter's wingspan, and when it was in range a red light would go on, signaling you to fire. It took me awhile to get used to the guns' noise and vibration as they were going off only about 3 or 4 inches from my head—on both sides. For years after the war, I had a mild hearing impairment. Not sure it ever really went away!

We were in Las Vegas for six weeks and only got into town once. During my gunnery training, I was made PFC [private first class] and got a little pay raise. But there wasn't much to spend it on; back then Las Vegas was one big dusty street and not a lot to do, nothing like it is today.

When I finished up gunnery school, I embarked on the last phase of my training, which started with another long train trip to Florida, where I would become even better acquainted with our B-17 and be assigned to a permanent crew at last.

I was excited by that prospect, but even more excited that they were allowing me a short leave so that I could transit to Florida with a stop at my hometown of St. Louis. That came as a surprise. I don't remember much about my trip back home except it was good seeing the folks and a few of my high school buddies and getting back on the tennis court a few times. The previous three months in the army, almost every moment of the day was accounted for, or planned for you, and then this break. So back to the old rituals, but everything was different now.

Those two weeks home went by very quickly, and then I had to say goodbye to Mom and Dad and to my grandpa and grandma who were living with them at the time. I was finally on my way to the war, and we all tried to put a brave face on it. Our big bombers were taking a beating over in Europe in the fall of 1943, heavy, heavy losses, and I think we knew that if it kept up like that, my chances of coming back home again were just so-so. The October newspaper headlines were full of that one Schweinfurt raid; we had lost sixty bombers and almost six hundred airmen in just one day trying to knock out the German ball-bearing plants. President

Roosevelt wanted the public to know about the price of war, the sacrifices the boys and their families were making, so there was no whitewashing Schweinfurt or the other heavy bomber losses that had preceded it. Word was out that the bomber crews weren't even surviving their first ten missions, and of course back then, it was twenty-five combat missions before you could come home. . . . So, my parents, well, they tried to be positive for my sake.

But it was one foot in front of the next, and before I knew it, I was back on the train and off to MacDill Field in Tampa, Florida, another long, long train ride. . . . And then meeting up with my crew, men that I would eventually go into combat with. That sure made things feel a lot more serious than before; we were now staging to go overseas and go right into the thick of it. We'd be replacing all those crews that were getting shot down. So, it was fly, fly, and fly some more.

In a short period of time, I got to know the boys on the crew, and we got all our routines down. I wasn't at MacDill very long before I got my promotion to staff sergeant and became a noncommissioned officer. That came along with a nice raise to $80 a month. When I was assigned to a combat crew, I also received another 50 percent bump, which came as a nice surprise. Pay was never anything that I gave much thought to during the war, but there it was. I was making more money than I had time to spend.

I don't want to give the impression that it was all just work, work, work at MacDill. They gave us some short breaks, and we hit those beautiful Florida beaches. My crew turned out to be a swell group of guys and we stuck together, officers and noncoms alike. We all came from very different places and backgrounds, and yet by the end of training, we fit together like a glove. While we were at MacDill, we spent a lot of time flying over the ocean. The main runway went right out over Tampa Bay. The coast of Florida was deserted back then, white beaches and low scrub and forest right along the coast, just a picture postcard. And a beautiful view from the ball turret.

Finally, in the late winter we went from MacDill Field to another base in Savannah, Georgia, where it was more of the same, but even more intense than before. Day after day we continued getting valuable time in the air, learning to work with each other, move about the plane with portable oxygen cannisters, simulating all sorts of emergencies and contingencies. Loss of power, loss of oxygen, how to deal with wounded on board. The navigator practiced navigating, the bombardier would drop bombs, and all of us gunners would fire at targets in the air. And there was constant drills and homework on aircraft identification, learning to quickly sort out the silhouettes of enemy and friendly fighter planes. Of course, you never wanted to hear, "Nice job, Sergeant; you just shot down one of our P-47s. Would you like to write the letter home to the pilot's family?"

Savannah was going to be our point of debarkation, so in late May we took off in a brand-new B-17G to a transit base in Maine and stayed overnight there. It was gorgeous country. From Maine we flew to Gander Bay, Newfoundland, for fueling. Essentially it was a great big rock, not a tree on it, and it was cold and windy.

Then we proceeded over the Atlantic, about nine hours, and landed in Ireland. It was just beautiful there; the foot-tall green grass was blowing and certainly looked welcoming after the long flight. We didn't stay there long; just refueled. We had been assigned to the 381st Bomb Group in Ridgewell, England.

Much to his surprise, when Bob's crew landed in England the end of May, they weren't sent directly on to the Ridgewell Airfield. Instead, they spent three weeks at an unnamed base (the location never made it through the censors). But Bob's two letters home from that base give a rare insight into life as a GI waiting to go into air combat:

June 8, 1944

Dear Mom and Dad,
I'm still here in England winning the war, pulling KP, guard duty and what have you. It is a very easy life though, so our complaints aren't justified. Now that D-Day has come, we're all a bit restless to get going, but our time will come soon enough, I guess.

A lot of WAACs arrived here. It was good to see some American Girls (coming from me, a WAAC disbeliever, that's pretty good). Last night Studee [Gene Studebaker] had guard duty around their quarters, keeping the soldiers out of range. A lot of them talk to us and give us candy bars that they had brought from the States, cake, etc. I honestly have to admit some were darn cute, a nicer-]looking bunch than I've ever seen. I even have a date with one of them tonight. There isn't much to do but go to the show here. It will be a lot of fun though because there aren't any other diversions here.

We are all getting over our restlessness now though we still have that old don't-give-a good-darn-about-anything which comes with idleness. Our rooms here are swell as is the chow. I guess I told you about that already.

A week later Bob wrote a second letter home:

June 15, 1944

Mom and Dad,

Here I am on the sack again. Tonight, I decided not to sweat out the long chow line, so I stopped in and had some tea and sandwiches at the tea shop down the road . . . I don't know how they drink that horrible stuff.

I'm anxious to get to my permanent base, which will be in about a week. We have good instruction here at this gunnery school. I'm learning more here than I have in all of my time in the States. All of our instructors are boys who just finished their missions. No bookwork here—just practical knowledge of everything we should know. So, a lot of helpful hints not in the books—knowledge learned the hard way—which I'm absorbing every word. Truthfully things look awfully good for me.

Our intelligence officer told us our mail will take about four more weeks after we hit our permanent field. God! They can't do this to me! But I'll just have to be patient.

Studebaker and I are studying up on our game of chess. We're becoming Wizards! We have some good battles anyway.

I finished *The Robe* several days ago. I forgot to tell you Mom it was the best book I've ever read. Certainly, enjoyed it.

I hope to have a chance to go to London. I'm dying to see a large town again.

Well, folks, not much more for now. I hope you are feeling fine. How's the garden, Mom? I'll write again soon, so until then.

All my love, Bob

Combat would arrive soon enough. Just two weeks later, Bob's crew would take to the air for their first flight over enemy-held territory. That combat mission, a milk run by all accounts, would open their eyes to the fickleness of fate in those frozen skies 5 miles above earth.

CHAPTER 3
FIRST COMBAT MISSION

Mission 1 June 28 Fismes, France 42-97589 unnamed B-17

On June 22, 1944, Bob Harper's crew joined the 381st Bomber Group, stationed at Ridgewell Airfield. During the four weeks prior to their arrival, the 381st BG had lost seventeen bombers and over one hundred men, starting with a disastrous strike on Berlin on May 24, when six of their thirty-seven bombers failed to return to base. I asked Bob for his memories of those first days at Ridgewell:

> The first night when we arrived at Ridgewell (June 22), we were assigned to the 533rd Squadron, and the five of us noncoms in my crew were sent to a Nissen hut. We were given the bunks of men who had been shot down the previous day and were now MIA [missing in action]. The crew's belongings hadn't been fully cleared out of the hut yet, and we were sleeping in their beds.* We could see the books that they had been reading. Extra clothes. Photos and newspaper clippings from back home, tacked up on the wall. The memory of that missing crew never left me. Suddenly it felt like we were living on borrowed time. . . . But we were trained to do the job, and we thought we knew what was coming. Turns out, we had no idea . . . not really.
>
> So, we began our life at Ridgewell inside that Nissen hut, which best resembles a tin can cut in half the long way and anchored to a concrete pad. The ends were made of wood, and there were the five of us in the hut, plus another crew of five. I was in a top bunk; I think the mattress was just straw ticking. The showers were about a couple hundred feet from us, and they were cold most of the time, but the chow hall was not too far away. Everything was kind of rough, but comfortable compared with what I'm sure the infantry and other soldiers had to put up with. We had a potbellied stove right in the middle of the hut. You would cook on one side and freeze on the other, but it kept it cozy. So that's where we stayed most of the time, especially later when the fall rains set in.

> That first week on base, I remember they kept us pretty busy. I don't recall exactly how many training missions we had to fly once we got over there to England, but with the close formations that were required, this orientation continued for most of that first week at Ridgewell. We had to learn to fly almost wing to wing while moving with the rest of the planes in formation. Of course, we were now waiting for that first combat mission. Maybe dreading it as well, considering we finally got to see some B-17s returning to Ridgewell damaged by flak. And we noticed how on edge everyone was. All around the base, bombers were being repaired, full of holes, or their engines being worked on. . . . I think you could say the mood there was somber, all business, trailers of live bombs being towed around. The crews kept to themselves for the most part. I guess it was a defensive mechanism that we picked up on right away . . . you know? Why bother to get to know anyone if they might not be around the next week. But that only made our crew grow closer.

The men of the 381st Bomber Group at Ridgewell were taken care of by the doctors and medical staff of the 242nd Medical Dispensary, whose members kept a daily diary detailing all medical issues, as well as recording a summary of missions, losses, and casualties. While researching Bob's story, I found this entry in the 242nd MD Diary, June 22, 1944, written on the same day that Bob and his crewmates arrived at Ridgewell. The previous day, three planes had failed to return from a bombing run to Berlin. After noting the names of the missing men and the fates of those three downed B-17s, the medical diary continued with an entry from Maj. Ernest Gaillard Jr., MD:

> Three (more) ships landed without hydraulics and two used parachutes to slow them down after they had landed. Lt. Schobert's ship had a failure of the hydraulic system as he was taxiing around the perimeter track, and he crashed into a fence near the bomb dump. Several ships had feathered props, and the battle damage to a number of ships is fairly heavy. Most of the damage was encountered by flak and fighters over the target (Berlin). The flak was intense and accurate.

* Most likely the bunks that Bob's crew settled into that first night at the Ridgewell Airfield were those of the men of the 533rd Squadron's B-17, "Baboon McGoon." On June 21, 1944, the "Baboon McGoon" ran into enemy fighters and was badly damaged. Two of her crew bailed out over Germany and were taken prisoner. Seven of her crew remained on board and were interned when the plane force-landed in Sweden.

> The morale of the crews is lower that it has been for many months. This is due to the decreased number of passes and the decrease in rest home facilities, the frequent change in the definition of an operational tour by higher command, the large number of missions flown in a comparatively short time, and the fact that many of the crew members are simply fatigued.
>
> We have had an increase in the number of cases that we have seen here showing anxiety reactions and feel that after today's mission the number we will see will be increased. Higher command a short time ago issued orders concerning pass and leave policies and at the same time issued operational orders which preclude carrying them out. It is felt that if some remedial action is not taken, the number of crew combat failures we have will increase.

Finally on June 28, 1944, after a week of orientation drills on the base, Bob's crew flew their first combat mission, bombing a strategic railway bridge in Fismes, France. Their unnamed B-17, 42-97589, was one of the thirty-six bombers from the 381st BG that rose into the sky that morning. As was standard practice in 1944, new crews flying into combat were piloted by an experienced officer for their first several missions. In Bob's case it would be with Lt. Ed Huber, with their regular pilot, 2Lt. Joe Pearce, relegated to the copilot seat. Of the nine men that Bob had trained with back in Florida, gunner Gene Studebaker and copilot Dale Winsor were assigned to other crews that day. Here's Bob's memory of his first combat mission:

> They roused us out of bed around 3:00 a.m. and sent us over for chow. We were each entitled to two fried eggs, real eggs not powdered eggs, for that mission-day breakfast, with ham or bacon. . . . Then we went out to the plane to install and check our guns and waited for the officers to get back from the briefing. All five of us gunners had zero combat experience; to say we were a little nervous would be an understatement. Still, when the pilots, navigator, and bombardier made it to the plane, we huddled up like a football team, and our new pilot, Ed Huber, calmly gave us the lowdown. Most of us were working on about four hours' sleep; we hadn't been told we were going out the next day . . . but we paid attention to every word.
>
> That Fismes mission turned out to be a milk run. Or at least they called it that. We flew as close to each other as we could to keep the fighters from flying through our formation, but we didn't

see any that day. Other than clearing my guns down in the ball turret, I didn't fire them again during the entire mission. Though it was light, the flak seemed accurate enough; some of those bursts of flak weren't too far from our plane. But the flak didn't last long; we dropped our bombs and then headed home. Everything was going perfectly.

But then I looked over at our wing man, and an 88 (artillery shell) had gone right through the tail gunner's position, blown off its left rudder. I can never forget the sight of those ammunition belts pulled straight out from the tail guns and flapping in the slipstream, flapping like crazy, like the tail of a kite. It happened near the French coast, so all the way back to England we could see those ammunition belts flapping . . . and we knew their gunner must have been hit. It was a shocking sight that stuck with me for a long time, those ammunition belts, and a hole where the gunner should have been. . . . But that damaged B-17 made it back to England and somehow managed to land at Ridgewell. I had heard tales of how durable our B-17 was, and now I was seeing it firsthand.

Back at base we went through debriefing, they gave us each a shot of whisky, and we talked briefly with a couple of intelligence officers. Then we went back, and we cleaned our guns. We hit the chow line, but I didn't have much of an appetite. I went and grabbed a quick shower, trying to rinse the day off, I guess, then went back to the hut and started a mission list. Number One, June 28, Fismes, France. I lay up in my bunk; the first mission hadn't been that bad. There was a part of me that thought, okay, one plane out of thirty-six was hit hard; one gunner out of 320 airmen was killed. Poor guy.

I got back down from my bunk and found that list and taped it up there next to my bed, along with a big map of Europe that I cut out of a newspaper. Then I circled Fismes on the map. One down and twenty-four to go! I decided that every time I made it back, I would add to the list and circle the target. Every time I circled it, I would be one mission closer to going home. I was dead-tired after my first mission. It hadn't been a long one, nothing like the long runs to Germany that I would fly soon enough, but the nervous tension of that first day was exhausting, and before long I managed to conk out.

The next day, Bob's crew was roused early again and went up with seven other planes in his squadron to join with hundreds of B-17s headed for Leipzig, Germany. But after crossing the English Channel, they were recalled due to bad weather. Bob didn't get credit for the mission despite flying for four hours. Here is the letter that he wrote home upon arriving back at the base, giving his family an update on life on base and his take on Army chow:

June 29, 1944

Dear Mom and Dad,

Oh, Happy Day—we had very bad weather, which meant no flying. Well, almost none; we flew for four hours at 28,000 feet and finally we had to abandon the mission because of clouds. That meant no raid and some much-needed sack time. I slept all afternoon without rolling over, and tonight I feel like a million dollars.

Every day I try and picture how things look at home this time of year. I can see a lot of warm summer days about now. How about that? And I bet your garden is really coming out, Mom. Have you many flowers or are they all vegetables?

Everything is going Okay over here, folks; nothing to worry about. I should be finished in several months. Won't that be wonderful! Possibilities of coming home are good—but first I'll have to stay here about three months instructing or something. I won't mind at all. Sweating out coming home will be a lot of fun. What I mean is that I'll be finished (with my missions) and can easily be patient.

All the fellows in the crew are fine. Studebaker has a slight cold and is resting. Nothing serious. We all fly together. These first few raids we will have a veteran pilot, and Joe Pearce flies as co-pilot. As soon as Joe is broken in enough, he'll be our first pilot again. I really like Lt. Pearce—we get along fine. Never forget the fun we had at Savannah Beach.

We keep Joe busy signing envelopes mass production like—in name or title—any officer can censor our letters—he will sign them anyway.

I can't get over the wonderful chow we have here. My gosh, it's just not army food! We have our own chow hall (combat crews). Every morning we either have fresh fried eggs or hot cakes (delicious) along with the daily choices of cereals, bacon, coffee, cocoa, and fruit. Just for example, here's lunch today; Pork chops, mashed potatoes and gravy, creamed corn, slice lettuce salad, carrots—dessert was cake with sauce over it.

Right now, I'm in the library of our Red Cross Aero club. Nothing elaborate but nice. These little things help out all. We have a record machine in the lounge, and the ladies have swell snacks prepared for us every night in the snack bar.

Haven't had any mail lately, but none has come through yet for any of us (direct). It will soon though. I enjoy your letters more than anything, Mom. Hope everything is going okay for you, Dad. I'm getting a little stale at cards, so you better take advantage of my idleness to practice up. Hmmm. Gulp.

A while back I had a few hours in Cambridge and had a look at the University. How beautiful it was—a mass of castles. This really is a foreign land alright [*sic*]. The downtown streets are real narrow. The bicycles can't seem to drive on the right side of the street—hard to get used to. The people dress fairly well, though everything is rationed. I can't even buy much-needed handkerchiefs.

I visited a pub (tavern). Like many of the elaborate imitation rathskellers in the States. Only this was the real thing! I can't stand their beer (warm—called bitters, mild ale, etc.).

I'm awful anxious to hear how my letters are coming through. Mom, I will write about every three days or so often as possible. The sack is a necessity here, not a luxury, and I can't write as often as I want to.

I'm surely thinking of you all a lot. I hope everything is swell at home. Hello to Joe and Grandma and Pa.

Lots of love, Bob

PS. Dad, the Cards and the Browns are really doing swell, aren't they? I look forward to our daily papers here with the scores."

Both of Bob's hometown teams, the St. Louis Cardinals and the St. Louis Browns, would meet in the World Series in October 1944, in what was called "the St. Louis Showdown." Bob and his crew would listen to those World Series games, which were broadcast on the radio to GIs all over the world. Returning from bombing runs deep into Germany on two occasions, Bob even managed to get back in time to be debriefed, get a bite to eat, and still catch a World Series game live.

The 1944 baseball season would also be known for the players who were not there, as well as for those who were playing. Many baseball stars had already been drafted, and the leagues were full of players in their late thirties and early forties who had come back out of retirement to fill the teams out, along with players quickly promoted from the minor leagues. But fans like Bob were happy to have a league at all, considering the world was at war:

> Listening to a World Series broadcast was like reaching out and touching my hometown again, you know? I had followed both St. Louis teams growing up. They even shared the same stadium, Sportsman's Park. I had gone to some of the games with my dad and grandpa and my brother Joe, so for me it was easy to imagine what was taking place.
>
> I'm not sure the actual baseball was a very high level that year, because so many talented players had been drafted by then. I think the Cardinals must have had a half-dozen players who were 4F or over forty. And the Browns had players either coming out of retirement or pulled up from the minor leagues. Anyway, it was a big deal for St. Louis, and I am sure the World Series was entertaining for everyone, a welcome distraction from the war for sure, even if just for a few hours. . . . They certainly were for me.

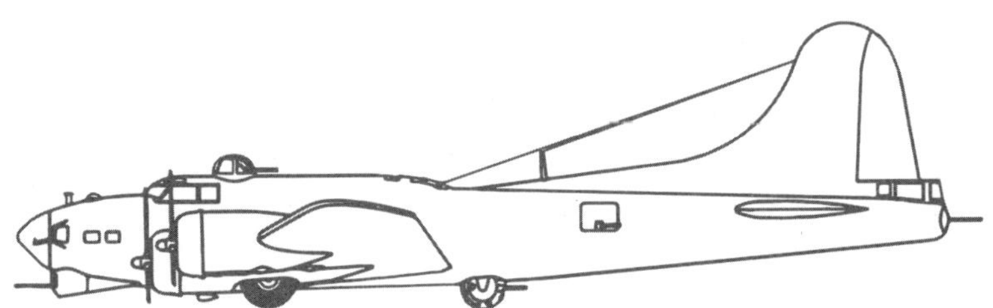

CHAPTER 4
JULY 1944: THIRTEEN COMBAT MISSIONS IN TWENTY-SIX DAYS

Mission 2	July 6	Rely, France	42-97357	"the Railroader"
Mission 3	July 7	Leipzig, Germany	42-97589	unnamed
Mission 4	July 8	Courbonne, France	42-97357	"the Railroader"
Mission 5	July 9	St. Omer, France	42-97357	"the Railroader"
Mission 6	July 12	Munich, Germany	42-97357	"the Railroader"
Mission 7	July 13	Munich, Germany	42-97357	"the Railroader"
Mission 8	July 16	Augsburg, Germany	42-40007	"Honey"
Mission 9	July 20	Dessau, Germany	42-97561	unnamed B-17
Mission 10	July 21	Schweinfurt, Germany	42-40007	"Honey"
Mission 11	July 25	St. Lô, France	42-40007	"Honey"
Mission 12	July 28	Merseburg, Germany	42-40007	"Honey"
Mission 13	July 29	Merseburg, Germany	42-40007	"Honey"
Mission 14	July 31	Munich, Germany	42-32025	"Dream Baby"

On June 6, 1944, the Allied forces invaded France, establishing multiple beachheads and opening the long-awaited Western Front on the European continent. As the German forces pushed back and attempted to reinforce their garrisons, the Allied air forces swung into action. For their part, the forty different American bomber groups of the 8th Air Force contributed heavily, often combining to send over a thousand bombers in daylight raids to attack enemy resupply lines. The 381st Bomber Group did their share as well, flying twenty-two missions in June and nineteen missions in July. It wasn't long before Bob and his crew were in the thick of it:

> I'm not sure any of us knew enough to appreciate those nine days of downtime, because we were all anxious to get our missions going and get home. . . . Then before we flew our second combat mission, we got some bad news. When we were busy back in the States finishing up combat training in Georgia, the 8th AF had raised the required combat missions to thirty from twenty-five. But no one told us about it! They informed us of that only after we got to Ridgewell. What a shock that was!

> But there wasn't a lot of time to dwell on the news because soon we were flying again, and it wasn't what we were expecting. They sent us out four straight days, one day after the other, with no down time, and that was tough for a new crew. Stressful. You'd hit the bunk at night not knowing if you'd get to sleep in the next morning or if someone was going to shake you awake in a couple of hours. No one ever said, "Better hit the rack; we're getting up early tomorrow." So, by that fourth day we were running on fumes. . . . And the third mission, that mission to Leipzig, was a doozy. It was our first flight into the enemy stronghold, and they let us know that we weren't welcome.

By all accounts, Bob's mission to Leipzig, Germany, was an eye-opener. On July 7, 1944, the 8th Air Force sent 1,129 bombers against various targets in the heavily defended Leipzig area, delivering a bomb payload of 2,200 tons onto synthetic oil plants, aircraft assembly plants and engine works, airfields, and railway targets. The bombers were stretched out in formations covering 40 miles of sky. Of those 1,129 bombers, 971 made it to their targets and dropped their ordinance. In the process, thirty-seven bombers (one in twenty-five) were shot down, and 390 bombers (one out of every three) returned battle damaged. Though the cloud cover was thick, a battle was raging all around Bob's 533rd Squadron, as other bomber groups fought off attacks from persistent German fighters. American escort fighters, a combined 756 P-38s, P-47s, and P-51s, claimed seventy-six German fighters while losing only six of their own.

Bob's recollection of the first time that his plane came under fighter attack also coincides with that mission to Leipzig. Leipzig was a heavily defended target with extensive antiaircraft emplacements, and the Leuna Oil Works in Merseburg wasn't far away. The area was critical to the German war effort and was defended by five Luftwaffe fighter fields.

> Some days, depending on where we were headed, if protecting the target was important enough to them, we would run into German fighters. They would leave you alone for a while, hold back, disappear into the clouds. Most of the time our "little buddies," the long-range P-51 fighters, escorted us in numbers large enough to discourage the German fighters . . . or at least to thin them out and break up their attacks. If for some reason our P-51 cover was needed elsewhere or if we didn't rendezvous with them as planned, the German fighters might show up as you left your bombing run, coming at

you out of nowhere. . . . Yeah, there is nothing as frightening as a Me 109 arcing towards you in a tight turn and suddenly his wings are blinking bright lights and you know he has you in his sights . . . and those winking lights are cannons.

I remember my first real encounter with a German fighter; we had been trained to shoot in short bursts, to keep the barrel from overheating but also to conserve ammo. I had only 400 rounds or so per gun, and the gun could fire 750 rounds per minute. But that first time, my training went out the window. Somewhere in the world there's a pair of .50-caliber machine guns that has my fingerprints on their triggers. From the day when I first realized that someone was trying to kill me . . . I just about emptied out my guns. And then I flew the rest of the mission with just a bit of ammo left. Just that one time . . . I guess I had to get it out of my system because it never happened again.

I interrupted Bob; it seemed the right time for this question: "Were you ever afraid up there?"

Afraid? Yes, sure. You betcha I was afraid! I think we all were. We all had our moments. But not as the mission started, at least not for me. Once we got up to 8,000–10,000 feet, I would climb down into the turret and rotate into position. So, I was now seeing the war from the belly of the B-17, and it was quite the viewpoint to have. The ball turret on the bottom of a Flying Fortress was a tiny thing, only 3 feet wide or so, pretty snug, but I fit in there okay. I sat on a piece of armor plate about 1 by 2 feet.

I had one of the best views of anyone on the plane; the belly turret had a lot of glass, and you could rotate it 360 degrees. On nice days, you could see forever, the beautiful clouds and the vapor trails from our bombers against this dark-blue sky. You could see the French and German countryside, farms and fields spread out below, so neat and orderly. Rivers and lakes sometimes sparkling in the sun. So peaceful. You could see the other B-17s boxed all around you. We flew in very close formation, making it harder for the German fighters to come through us . . . so you could even see some of the other crews. And you could see the bombs falling from where I sat . . . and then smoke coming up from the target. We hit the oil storage works in Hamburg once, and the smoke must have rose to 30,000 feet. You could see it almost all the way back to England.

But next to the pilots and bombardier, I think I also had the best view of the flak [exploding German antiaircraft shells]. When you got closer to the target, you could no longer vector around the antiaircraft emplacements, especially on your final bombing run . . . there was nothing peaceful about that . . . there was the sight of flak exploding all around you. Some days our ride was smooth, but other days it was like being tied to the belly of a bucking horse; the plane jerked all around, the pilots doing what they could to avoid other planes that were also avoiding other planes that may have been hit or just coming out of the clouds right into our own squadron. . . . But the sight of flak walking towards you, an illusion because you were actually flying into it at 180 mph or so, was the worst . . . red explosions followed by thick, black puffs, sometimes so thick you felt there was no avoiding them . . . because below you, the German gunners were trying to dial in your elevation. . . . I hate to say it, but at that point we were basically helpless, and we all knew it. The pilot had to hold the bomb run no matter what . . . sometimes for ten straight minutes even if we were getting pounded. . . . I don't remember which mission it was, but I remember one afternoon taking a terrible pounding, and my turret took a hit. When we got back, I removed a 3-inch piece of flak that came through and got lodged in the glass. I don't know how it missed me, being as I took up most of the room in that little ball turret. . . . I kept that piece of flak for years, though I have no idea where it is now.

Yes, so making that bombing run could feel like an eternity. . . . Then the bombs were finally released, and the plane soared up, 6,000 pounds lighter, and banked away. At that point we were only interested in escaping the flak, getting the heck out of there. The plane had indicators to tell the pilots that the release was clean, and other ones to tell them that the bomb doors were back up and closed, but Joe [Lt. Pearce] was a careful pilot, and he always wanted to hear from us that we had visuals, that the racks were clear, none of the bombs hung up, and the doors shut tight.

Sorry; back to your question. Sure, we were all afraid. But for most of us, I think it was a question of not wanting to let the team down, not letting your crewmates and friends down. So, we all stayed steady and did our jobs the best we could. We never talked about it, but I feel sure we were all in the same boat when it came to wondering if somehow, we would make it through our thirty

> missions. . . . And then just a few weeks after we found out about that increase to thirty missions, we got the word that our required missions had been raised again by five. Now we were going to have to fly thirty-five combat missions. We were in disbelief . . . utter disbelief. I'll tell you more about that later.

I took the opportunity to ask Bob a follow-up question: "Bob, there was a lot of talk about belly-turret gunners not wearing their parachutes or not being able to fit them down there in the belly turret. Can you give some firsthand input on that?":

> It was tight in there, so I never brought my parachute in the turret during the training missions. Even when we started flying combat, I didn't at first. I kept it hanging up in the fuselage at the ready, but I would have to be rotated up and get out of the turret, then put it on. And during combat, our B-17 could absorb so much damage so quickly that there might not be enough time or warning for me to get out of the turret, hook that parachute on, and then find my way to the waist door to jump.
>
> Then I had an experience that changed my mind about bringing my parachute down into the ball turret with me. I couldn't tell you which exact mission this happened on, but it might have been the one to Leipzig that you mentioned. Somewhere a B-17 in a formation forward and high above our squadron got hit and exploded, and their ball turret detached and went flying right by us, along with other pieces of that B-17. Just for a split second, I thought I spotted that poor gunner still in there, but he wasn't trying to get out of the turret. Then he was gone, just a speck far below us. I figured he probably didn't have his chute with him.
>
> When we got back to Ridgewell, I asked Joe Pearce, our pilot, would it be okay if I took a parachute down in the turret with me? He said, "Sure, Shorty, just as long as it doesn't interfere with your guns." So, I got one of the smaller chest parachutes that hooked to two rings on the front of your chute harness, and then attached it to the right harness ring, and once I got into the turret, I would swing it over to the side. That made things even tighter down there, but I sure felt better. I had a hatch behind me, and now with my parachute, I might be able to get out if there wasn't time to rotate the turret up, or if something went wrong with that.

Those first missions, we saw a few planes go down in the distance and their crews parachuting, so we began to prepare mentally for that possibility. You know, you counted the parachutes coming out of those damaged bombers if you could, but you had a lot of things on your mind and you had to keep on task. When you got debriefed after the mission, you were asked if you saw any parachutes, when and where, and so it's not like you could block it out. . . . Afterwards, you tried not to dwell on it, the guys that didn't make it out and went down with their planes. . . . You know, it didn't have to be your own squadron or even bomber group; you could see a bomber explode miles away, and it was like it was happening right next to you. Or watch one slowly spin in the far distance, smoking, knowing they weren't going to pull out. We didn't talk about it, but it was there in the back of your mind. I think we all mentally rehearsed an escape plan if our plane was disabled. And hoped we could survive it . . . we just didn't talk about it much.

After those four back-to-back missions, we got a few days off and then we flew two missions to Munich, two days in a row on July 12 and 13; those were long flights, tough missions. I think the Germans were slowly coming to grips with the fact that we had successfully invaded France, and now we were occasionally seeing fighters.

Thinking back, of course, the flights to Germany were the worst. We would get to the plane in the morning while the officers were at the mission briefing, still dark out. We'd install and check the guns and get organized. We also checked the bomb bay to see if we had a fuel bladder on board, a big black plastic bladder which would extend our range. If it was there, well, we knew we were headed to Germany. We'd climb back down when we heard the jeep coming with our officers. We knew them really well by then, and we could tell from the looks on their faces if they thought we had a tough one ahead. Honestly? For us, it was always a big gulp; oh, no, Germany again. And then we would kind of laugh and try to make a joke of it.

Those first days at Ridgewell in June and July, the air base was buzzing with the D-day invasion, and everyone wanted to do what they could to help the troops on the ground. Thirteen combat missions in just twenty-six days was tiring, exhausting, but I guess we would have flown every day if they asked us to.

On the positive side, I remember thinking in July that at the rate we were flying, even with the increase to thirty-five, I might finish up my missions by the end of September and be home for Christmas, the latest. Boy, I had that all wrong.

At first, Bob's crew flew mostly on the B-17G, "the Railroader," but on mission number 8, on July 16, 1944, Bob's crew flew to Augsburg, Germany, on a B-17G number 42-40007, named "Honey." "Honey" would quickly become Bob's favorite plane, but not that first day. That first mission on "Honey" would be one of the strangest and most unsettling of his thirty-five:

> We were taxiing towards the runway, in a long line of B-17s, and suddenly Fleming jumped out the waist door and started running. He was part of our original crew, a gunner who had trained with us in Florida and Georgia . . . we couldn't believe our eyes.

Up next is the story of the man who ran and the one who could have walked away.

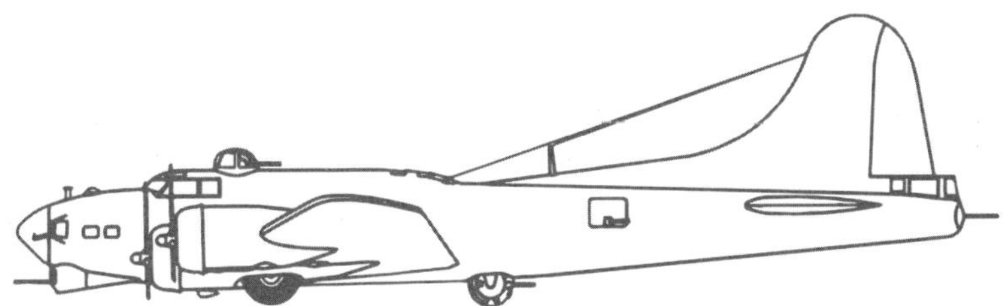

CHAPTER 5
THE MAN WHO RAN AND THE ONE WHO COULD HAVE WALKED AWAY

Mission 8 July 16,1944 Augsburg, Germany 42-40007 "Honey"

On July 16, 1944, Bob and the four other sergeants that made up his crew finished installing their guns. Then they gathered beneath the B-17 420007, known as "Honey," and waited for the officers to arrive from the mission briefing. A few minutes later, a jeep pulled up, and out jumped Lieutenants Pearce, Winsor, Yolofsky, and Weisser. The crew huddled up briefly near the bomb bay doors, and the pilot, 2Lt. Joe Pearce, quickly outlined the coming trip to Augsburg, Germany: route to target, expected flight time, fighter coverage, and expected locations along the flight path where they might run into flak and enemy fighters. Then he looked around the crew to see if there were any questions.

"Everyone got it? Okay, let's make it a good one," Pearce added in his normal, confident voice. Then he turned away from the men and signaled to the crew chief, and the two men did a slow walk around the bomber, making one last inspection while the men boarded. Finally, Pearce climbed aboard "Honey." As the engines fired up, the crew went through their checklists once again. It was their eighth combat mission together, and prepping their bomber went smoothly.

"Nothing seemed any different that morning," Bob told me. "None of us suspected that Fleming was going to jump out and make a run for it."

The story that followed sounded oddly familiar to me. A few minutes after I got off the phone with Bob, I finally recalled why. When I was fifteen years old, the famous Civil War novel by the American writer Stephen Crane, *The Red Badge of Courage*, had been required reading for all high school sophomores in New York State's public school system. In Crane's tale, a young man volunteers in the Union army in the early days of the American Civil War. Soon after his enlistment, this "Youth" begins to struggle with thoughts of the coming battle, wondering how he will fare and fearing that he won't hold up. He attempts to get his fellow soldiers talking about courage, hoping to find comfort in similar fears and doubts:

> The Youth watched him for a moment in silence. When he finally spoke, his voice was as bitter as dregs. "Oh, you're going to do great things, I s'pose!"
>
> The loud soldier blew a thoughtful cloud of smoke from his pipe. "Oh, I don't know," he remarked with dignity; "I don't know. I s'pose I'll do as well as the rest. I'm going to try like thunder." He evidently complimented himself upon the modesty of this statement.
>
> "How do you know you won't run when the time comes?" asked the Youth.
>
> "Run?" said the loud one; "run? Of course not!" He laughed.
>
> "Well," continued the Youth, "lots of good-a-'nough men have thought they was going to do great things before the fight, but when the time come, they skedaddled."
>
> "Oh, that's all true, I s'pose," replied the other; "but I'm not going to skedaddle. The man that bets on my running will lose his money, that's all." He nodded confidently.

The Youth finally goes into combat, remaining steadfast and brave for the first few hours. When the Rebel troops break through nearby, he sees some Union troops starting to run and he panics, fleeing the scene. Then in the confusion of the battle, the Youth wanders around in the rear of the Union position, eventually joining a column of wounded men with bloody bandages. He sees their bandages as "red badges of courage" and wishes he had one. Eventually the Youth is accidentally injured by a fellow deserter. With his own forehead now bloodied, the Youth finds his way back to his own outfit. Believing that the Youth had been lost in combat, his squad members welcome him back joyfully, glad to see that his wounds were only minor. With his episode of cowardice out of the way, the young soldier goes on to fight bravely, even serving as the standard-bearer for his unit in a battle the next day.

Eighty years after the American Civil War ended, we have Bob's story, similar in ways but with a different outcome. After researching Fleming's desertion for additional documentation, I telephoned Bob, and we discussed his crewmate:

> Yeah, Fleming? Who knows? They had upped the missions on us again; that didn't help. And as you said, we had flown six missions in eight days and that was stressful, I suppose. And then, none of

> us were operating on a lot of sleep. We had a few days off, then we got the call to go to Augsburg, Germany. We had been to Munich on our last two missions, long flights, back to back, and Augsburg was just a few miles short of there. So, it could have been another tough mission ahead of us.
>
> We were taxiing towards the runway, in a long line of B-17s, and suddenly Fleming jumped out the waist door and started running. He was part of our original crew, a gunner who had trained with us in Florida and Georgia. . . . We couldn't believe our eyes . . . Joe Pearce was the pilot, and he radioed the tower and asked if he should abort. They told him to just get on with it, so we left Ridgewell short one gunner. I guess Fleming just chose that moment to crack.

Digging through the official crew lists of Bob's missions as well as the combat diaries of the 533rd Squadron and the 381st Bomber Group, I discovered that Fleming had served as a waist gunner on all seven of his previous combat missions. On the day that Fleming deserted the bomber, he was listed for the first time as the tail gunner. He had also flown with Bob on that first mission to Fismes and, like Bob, had witnessed that tail gunner being killed in the B-17 on their wing. I wondered if that might have influenced Fleming, and asked Bob about that possibility.

"Maybe that was it," Bob replied. "Anyway, someone shifted to the tail turret gun, and we flew that morning with just eight men. It turned out that the mission to Augsburg wasn't bad at all. Not much flak. We didn't see any fighters. All our planes made it back . . . one of the milk runs that you hoped for."

I asked Bob about the consequences for Fleming, expecting to hear that he had been court-martialed for deserting the bomber.

"No, no court-martial that I ever heard of," Bob told me. "But Fleming got busted down to private and was assigned to KP. He worked in the kitchen over at the noncom's mess. Seemed happy as could be whenever we ran into him, but we didn't have much to do with him afterwards. We were living in different worlds, I suppose. We weren't unfriendly or anything . . . I mean we would say hello, but that was it."

I found an entrance in the 533rd combat diary confirming Fleming's demotion to private a week later, but nothing about the circumstances. I also found a brief mention of it in a letter that Bob sent home, dated July 26, 1944: "Fleming is on KP now, so he won't be with us for a week or so. He talked back to a captain the other day and it went pretty bad for him. He's a private now."

When I ran that by Bob, he explained the circumstances. "I couldn't tell Mom and Dad what really happened. One of the crew deserting our B-17? It would have worried them. And when I wrote that note, we still had no idea if Fleming was coming back or what would happen to him."

Later, I had the chance to interview the pilot's nephew, Robert Pearce, and Robert provided an even more detailed account of that mission and the consequences for Fleming:

> My Uncle Joe (pilot, Lt. Pearce) told me about that day. Uncle Joe still had most of his original crew together, the same crew that had trained together in the States, and they were headed out on a mission to Germany. As they approached takeoff, the crew told him that Fleming had jumped out of the waist door and was running back towards quarters. My uncle contacted the tower to let them know that they had lost a gunner, and they told him to proceed anyway to takeoff.
>
> Early the next morning, Fleming came to Uncle Joe to apologize. He couldn't explain what had happened. And now he just wanted to get back with the old crew and fly again. But my uncle told him to give it a few days; he needed to think about it. So, Fleming went to some of the other pilots instead, asking to fly with them. No one would have him. Then Fleming came back to Uncle Joe a couple of days later and begged him to let him fly again with his old crew. To put in a good word for him with the higher-ups. But Uncle Joe had to refuse him because he felt he could no longer trust him. My uncle told me it was one of the toughest decisions that he had to make during all those months of combat . . . because he knew he was Fleming's only chance to fly again. But he just couldn't chance Fleming freezing up during a combat mission. He couldn't risk the lives of the crew. So, he had to say no.

On July 23, Fleming was busted down to private and spent the rest of his war working in the mess hall. His pay was cut more than two-thirds in the process, back down to a private's $50 a month, with combat and flight pay suspended as well. When the war ended, he made it back to California and had a family and lived into his eighties. For those Civil War historians among you, you have already figured out that Henry Fleming was not his real name (Henry Fleming is the name of the youth in *Red Badge of Courage*). Bob's crewmate *Fleming* didn't run in his first battle; he lasted through seven of them. In light of that, I decided to grant him the anonymity that Fleming earned with his seven combat missions.

But his story stuck with me and inspired me to do some further research. Most of us who have studied war and soldiers in combat know that individual courage in battle is a difficult thing to predict. It was true in the American Civil War, it was true in ancient Greece, and it was true in the trenches of World War I. At the outbreak of World War II, those who managed the American effort knew it as well. Hoping to determine who might be more susceptible to cracking under duress, especially under prolonged periods of stress, the Army Air Force created elaborate screening tests for all air force candidates, including performing some complicated physical and mental games and puzzles while surrounded with noise and distractions (one pilot candidate recalled someone banging a pot over his head while he was solving math equations). But with so many men being screened, a psychiatric evaluation could also be as simple as the candidate having a short chat with the interviewing psychiatrist.

Of course, what followed, the grueling training that the men went through in their subsequent aviation and gunnery schools (up to a year, depending on the position), was also guaranteed to weed out those who could not handle the stress that came with the job in the rarefied atmosphere 5 miles above the earth. Though many of the accidents that occurred during the training period stateside could be attributed to weather or equipment failure, some were the results of judgment errors made under the stress of split-second decisions. And the numbers of accidents, not shared during wartime, was substantial. According to the AAF Statistical Digest printed after the war, in the period December 1941–August 1945, the US Army Air Forces lost 14,903 pilots, aircrew, and assorted personnel plus 13,873 airplanes while training and operating *inside* the continental United States, the result of 52,651 aircraft accidents (6,039 involving fatalities).

But as they say, there is no substitute for the real thing, and when these well-trained airmen left their training regimens and entered combat, the next level of stress began. Accidents were now just one of the possible outcomes of flying. The vast network of German air defenses, unpredictable and dangerous, had to be faced day after day. Incidents of nervous breakdowns and crack-ups during the 8th Air Force combat tours were not rare. "Flak happy" entered the vocabulary of those who fought in the skies. Airmen, including Bob, joked about it. Then there was the next level of flak happy: incapacitating shaking hands, nervous tics, onset of hypochondria, refusal to board the bombers, or inability to function during missions. Steps were formulated to ameliorate the effects of this combat stress, to get ahead of it, but base commanders were also under pressure to keep the bombers in the air, and their approaches varied throughout the forty different US bomber groups operating in England.

In an attempt to keep the airmen flying and decrease the incidence of airmen becoming "flak happy," the base commanders had a few options: they could rotate men in the schedule and, when possible, issue two- or three-day passes so that they could get off base. This could be extended to a weeklong visit at a flak hotel (Bob's crew will visit one in a later chapter, but not for two months after the episode with Fleming). More-drastic steps were often taken with airmen who suffered complete breakdowns (especially pilots whose longer training period moved them up to the status of "too valuable" to lose). Instead of flak hotels, the severe cases went off to "flak hospitals," where they could be subject to seventy-two hours of narcotherapy and sedation to "reset" these temporarily (it was hoped) incapacitated men. Reset them, but not so that they could be sent home with lighter duties, but rather so that they could be sent back to combat. As more flying officers became available in 1944, that practice was discontinued, and flak hospitals were more often stopovers for combat-stressed pilots on their way back to the States, where they might finish their service as flight instructors or take on nonflying duties.

Though the word "flak" became part of the everyday parlance of the English-speaking men who flew and worked on the big bombers, it originated as a contraction of the German word **FL**ieger**A**bwer**K**anone, which translates to "flyer defense cannon" or what the Allies would refer to as antiaircraft guns. In slang, flak referred specifically to the thousands of steel shards from the exploding shells from these cannons, which would wreak havoc as they penetrated the thin aluminum skins of the B-17s and B-24s. In the last half of 1944, while Bob was flying with the 381st BG, the large bomber losses in the European theater of operations (ETO) totaled 1,562. Of those bomber losses, 978 were attributed to flak (392 to fighters and 192 to collisions and other accidents).

But many B-17s also survived being hit by hundreds of pieces of flak. One of the best examples of the B-17's durability was "Little Miss Mischief," a B-17 with the 91st BG, stationed at Bassingbourn, about 30 miles from the Ridgewell base. On October 15, 1944, the "Little Miss Mischief" took a direct flak burst and an estimated one thousand pieces of flak penetrated midway down the fuselage. Though the belly turret was shredded, its gunner miraculously survived the explosion, only to have to stay down there (and suffer frostbite) until the plane managed to safely land back at base and he could be extracted. A photo of the "Little Miss Mischief" can be seen in the photo section, one of the many examples of badly flak-damaged B-17s that made it back to their bases despite receiving near catastrophic damage."

Eventually, I asked Bob what caused the most stress during his tour of combat. His answer surprised me:

Obviously, flying into some of those flak fields was stressful for all of us. Those long, back-to-back missions with no rest in between also took their toll. There were lots of images that we carried with us of combat that were hard to forget . . . but there was one thing that really played havoc with our nerves when we first got to Ridgewell: the moving of the goal posts when they increased the required missions on us.

When I was selected for aerial gunnery school in the fall of 1943, I was told it would be twenty-five combat missions for our bomber crews, and then we would either be sent home to the States or given noncombat duties, most likely using our combat experience to train the new crews that were arriving in England. So mentally, that is what we signed up for. Twenty-five missions, and that was bad enough because most crews in 1943 weren't surviving fifteen. Once we were over in England and in combat, trust me, every single one of us counted and kept track of those missions. Some of the guys, like me, put a map on the wall and circled their mission targets, numbering them. Others kept diaries or journals. We might not talk too much about it; no one wanted to jinx themselves or anyone else, but mission count was always on your mind.

As I mentioned before, shortly after we arrived and began flying combat, we found out our combat tour had been raised to thirty missions. I don't remember the specific day, but someone in the hut said, "You're not gonna believe this, but we are supposed to fly thirty now. They say it's been that way since back in April or May." I guess we were the last ones to be told. Welcome to the Army.

And not much later, it couldn't have been more than two or three weeks, so it was sometime in July, I remember returning from a long, difficult mission to Germany, one of the challenging ones because I was exhausted and just wanted to get some chow and close my eyes and hit the sack. Studebaker said, "Here they go again . . . they've added another five missions. Now it's up to thirty-five." I sat down on a bunk in disbelief. I just couldn't believe my ears. Some general had made up his mind to make our lives that much harder. To lessen our chances of surviving the war. . . . What was to keep them from raising the missions to forty or fifty? None of us had the answer to that.

You might think the officers would have been given more information, but they were in the dark as well. So that added an element of stress for sure. It was also a little demoralizing. Someone in the hut joked, "I'm going to need a bigger map," but no one laughed. We made the best of it as usual. After they changed it to thirty-five, they never raised it again. But they never told us they wouldn't, either. Welcome to the Army.

Bob had raised an interesting issue about the length of combat tours. I took a look into it and found a surprising scarcity of information on the topic. Unlike with so many other aspects of the war, the 8th AF never released much information on those decisions, even in the massive postwar studies and reports that they commissioned. What I did find was that while Bob and the rest of the Pearce crew were completing their final training in Georgia in the spring of 1944, Gen. Jimmy Doolittle, commander of the 8th Air Force, raised the required combat missions from twenty-five to thirty for all heavy-bomber groups stationed in England.

Earlier in the war, the Supreme Command gave each of the Army Air Force commands the authority to regulate combat tours for their airmen, so Gen. Doolittle was in his rights to do so. As the long-range fighter escort program became effective and American bomber losses dropped, General Doolittle had used those new statistics to keep his experienced bomber crews in Europe for as long as possible, allowing the 8th AF to fly a record number of sorties in April, May, and June in anticipation of the D-day invasion, and to have the crews on hand to follow up in July in support of the Allied troops on the ground in France.

But for the men completing their twenty-five missions after Doolittle's directive that spring, it was the bitterest of feelings. The long-range fighter escort was helping their survival rates on average, but the bombers still were often subject to fierce German fighter attacks and the strengthened flak defenses, so heavy losses were not uncommon. Some argued that every man who was lost between missions 26 and 30 was an "unnecessary tragedy" for families waiting at home to see their sons again. For a while the sarcastic refrain circulated the 8th Air Force Bases: "We do twenty-five for ourselves and country, and five for Jimmy [Doolittle]."

The summer after Doolittle's spring edict, the required missions were raised again, this time to thirty-five. The men that went into combat believing they had to survive twenty-five missions now had to adjust to the fact that it had been increased by 40 percent. This subject would eventually be written about in great length in *Catch-22*, a postwar novel by Joseph Heller.*

* Heller's famous novel *Catch-22* is the story of Capt. Yossarian, a fictitious bombardier flying with an American bomber group stationed on an island near Italy during World War II. Yossarian's commanding officer, Col. Cathcart, trying to curry favor with the upper command, keeps increasing the number of required missions that his crews must fly, and volunteering them for dangerous ones as well. The bomber crews work out the stress and uncertainty of these increased tours with both tragic and humorous results. Joseph Heller wrote from firsthand experience, having flown sixty missions as a B-24 bombardier with the 12th AF, 340th BG, out of Italy.

THE MAN WHO COULD HAVE WALKED AWAY

Unlike Fleming, most airmen fighting with the 8th Air Force managed to keep it together, and many distinguished themselves admirably under incredible strain. Though numerous stories of the individual heroics of those bomber crews have been written, there were also many instances of quiet bravery on display. Every day. One of Bob Harper's crewmates, Sgt. Bruce Bentley, was a perfect example of this quiet determination. Bruce was a man who could have begged off combat duty but who chose to stay and fly with his crewmates. Harper:

> Speaking of courage, I just want to take a moment here and tell you about my friend, our radio operator, Bruce Bentley. We all had moments of nauseousness at first, flying those B-17s. Motion sickness, altitude sickness, the constant cold, sometimes −40°F or worse. Imagine being close to sea level one moment, then two or three hours later you were flying at 28,000 feet, your oxygen mask frozen to your face, breaking off the ice every five minutes or so. The B-17s weren't pressurized, and even with that oxygen you could feel it, for some of us, a perpetual mild headache. Then there were clogged ears; pretty darn painful, but something that became less frequent as we trained. Your body adjusts. We were young men and in great shape. But Bruce got airsick every time he went up; he would wind up vomiting, get sick as a dog. He made us all promise not to mention it, not to discuss it outside the crew.
>
> Bruce's airsickness was one of those cases where it was so chronic and severe that the doctors probably would have permanently grounded him. But Bruce didn't want to let the rest of us down, and he was determined to do his thirty-five missions, so we kept it to ourselves. He would vomit into a bucket that he brought along and then take care of it somewhere along the way. By the time we hit the coast of France, he was feeling good enough to do his job. Bruce always pulled his weight, and we knew we could count on him.
>
> The elevation also played havoc with your sinuses, and some of us got chronic sinusitis. You know, when you go up in an aircraft and there is no way of controlling the cabin pressure. That was rough. So occasionally we would get sick with these head colds and stay sick for a while, but we usually avoided going to sick bay so we could fly together and get these required missions over with. . . . There was a premium on handkerchiefs, that's for sure, because I remember them being hard to find, and writing my mom, asking her to send me some.

> But I think back to Bruce sometimes; he could have gotten out of combat, but he insisted on coming along. None of us—well, with that one major exception—ever let the other guys down. To this day, I never think about Fleming, one way or another. I don't judge him. If he didn't want to be up there that badly, it was better that he wasn't. . . . Still, if I close my eyes, I can see him running across the field—he quit; he just couldn't handle it. What more can I say?
>
> Thinking back, July was a rough month, all those missions piled one on top of the next. But we did get a three-day pass in the middle of July and headed to London . . . and that was a pretty amazing experience!

Having "skedaddled," Fleming would be confined to the base and miss that trip to London. He would also "miss" the additional (now twenty-seven) combat missions that he had signed up for and avoid being shot down four months later with the rest of the crew.

CHAPTER 6
OFF TO WARTIME LONDON

In the middle of July 1944, Bob and his crew were suddenly granted a short leave. Between his letters home and his postwar journal, Bob provides a GI's perspective as he travels through London, a city still recuperating from the Blitz:

> I don't know whether it was because of Fleming taking a powder that morning, but when we got back from that mission to Augsburg, we got the news that our crew was getting a two-day pass so the next day we headed to London by train. Gene Studebaker and I travelled together that first trip. The tallest man on the base and the shortest; we made quite the pair.
>
> Of course, money didn't mean anything to us in those days. I was making about $200 a month, which was about the equivalent to a British colonel. On that first trip we grabbed the first rooms we could find. However, on our next visit we stayed at the second-best hotel, the Regent Palace on Piccadilly Square, very expensive, where the tourists stayed. The Savoy was the top hotel, down the street a couple of blocks. We were just spending money; we didn't worry about that. When we ran out, we ran out. Eventually we found a nice little hotel over on Russsell Square called the Imperial, and that was about a fifth of the cost and not in the tourist area.
>
> Those trips to London and Cambridge were really special and all started with a train ride. Once we got there, most of our traveling in London was by the underground. The cabs had shades over their headlights, which would eliminate about 90 percent of the light as seen from above. There were no streetlights, no lights visible from the houses, or hotels, or anything. At night we'd get on the underground, and London at that time was completely blacked out. We'd get off the underground, go up at any stop, not knowing where we were, get out in the total blackness and look for a building that had a light under the door. Almost always, they'd be pubs! So, we'd go in and drink their mild and bitters beer, which wasn't highly carbonated, typical of English beer.
>
> The beer barrels were put in the basement; they didn't have any refrigeration systems. They would pipe the beer upstairs to the

bar, so it was not real cold. We played darts with the English people, who treated us really well; they appreciated us coming over there. Some of the guys from our base did have trouble with the English soldiers on occasion, they thought we were hot-shots, and we made so much more money than they did. Every once in a while, we'd get in a little fracas, but all-in-all my crew never had any trouble and were just tickled to get away from the base.

I'll never forget, one day I went shopping on, I think it was Oxford Street, I seem to remember it was the famous shopping street. . . . I went in this fancy department store and saw an ash tray, which was plated silver, with a B-17 and cost 40 pounds. A small fortune, but to this day I regret that I didn't buy it.

A letter home detailing Bob's trip offers an eyewitness view of the city. Written on the train while on the way back to the base from London, it's a time capsule from war-torn London:

July 19, 1944, Wednesday

Dear Mom and Dad,

Studebaker and I are now in Cambridge on our way back from London, where we spent our two-day pass. I have so much to tell you all I hardly know where to start, but I'll do my best and try to mention the most interesting parts of our travels . . . Hmmm . . .

I didn't have to wait long to see my first ruins left by the Blitz in 1940, because the train passed through some of the worst on our way into the station. Well, it's just as pictures show it. Some buildings that were damaged beyond repair were torn down, while others were only slightly damaged. The poor business district was almost razed by the bombing on Dec. 29th, 1940. It's a crime.*

We didn't arrive in town early enough to get in a good hotel, so we ended up in a once beautiful hotel, which now only has a few usable rooms. Not bad but a bit antique and dirty due to the lack of upkeep.

We, being complete strangers, thought that the best idea to see some of the sights was to rent a cab. So that's exactly what we did the next day, and our driver took us on a tour of the most well-known places. It turned out swell because our driver was a smart and witty fellow. Enclosed is a list of the places we saw.

Before I forget, folks, I want to explain that most of the city is still intact. Of course, there isn't hardly a building untouched by bombs, but mostly just slight damage done, making the majority of the historical sites we saw still in good shape. I'm sorry mom that I couldn't get any literature on the art we saw, just none to be had except at Westminster Abbey and I'm going to mail you the book I was able to purchase there. I really enjoyed it and know you will too.

The Abbey is a beautiful church alright [*sic*], and the slight bomb damage that was done has been repaired. Our guide told us the history of the place, all about the men whose ashes are left under the gravestones on the floor. The Abbey is more of a graveyard for royalty and poets than for anything else. They hold church services daily for those who care to attend. The King and Queen go once in a while. The altar where the coronation is held is beautiful, as is the whole cathedral. The only American buried in the Abbey is Peabody, other than that just about every King and English Poet I've ever heard of is there.

Saint Paul's cathedral has been hit by two bombs but not too much damage was done. It stands out like a sore thumb amongst the old business district that I mentioned was almost leveled to the ground by bombs in 1940. A real miracle how the bombs landed all the round the cathedral, with only two of them hitting. Mostly great warriors and soldiers are buried in the Cathedral. I recognize so many that it would take pages to list them, but Lawrence of Arabia, and Sir George Williams, the founder of the YMCA, came as a surprise to me. St. Paul's has the second-largest dome in the world, beautiful paintings and mosaic work and its whispering tower makes it look a lot like the one in the capital [*sic*] in Washington. St. Paul's and Westminster Abbey are just a couple of the wonderful sights that we took in.

Gad, folks, are you still awake?

At night I rode in the "tubes" or "undergrounds," what we call subways. And can you imagine, they are still packed with women and children. Everyone who must have been bombed out at some time or another sleeps in the undergrounds, which are very deep below the surface (very modern and speedy escalators and elevators take you down) and serve as air raid centers.

There are so many good plays showing (and I wanted to see them all at once). I chose *The Blithe Spirit*,** and boy was it good! The theater itself is classy, and I mean as modern as any I've ever seen. It had two bars that served tea between acts. The play was funny as could be. The English humor is certainly up to date.

Yesterday Studebaker and I met up with our crew at the Regent Palace, where they are staying. It's on Piccadilly Circus. Really nice. Saw the Tower of London today in great detail, what an experience. Don't forget to ask me about it when I get home.

Well, the buzz bombs, doodle bugs or robot bombs, didn't come near me during our visit. They are bad though. It is a terrible feeling for the people who live there, not knowing what they might come home to after work at night. They land all over. Whoops, time to get on the train. To be Continued . . .

The morning following Bob's return to base, he got up before dawn and flew a long combat mission to bomb the enemy aircraft engine factories in Dessau, Germany. Of the 8th Air Force's 417 B-17s that were sent out on targets that day, fifteen of them, or one out of every twenty-five, were shot down, and a whopping 45 percent of them returned battle-damaged. Though the 381st Bomber Group escaped any losses, they received their share of damage from the flak and fighters. When Bob got back to his barracks that night, he finished up that letter home, not giving any details of the mission, just mentioning that he had "worked" that day:

Continued . . . Well, Mom and Dad, I'm tired now and don't feel as if I can write well at the moment . . . Had to work today. And Mom, you're wonderful. I came back [from the combat mission] to 3 more letters and a V-mail from the 15th waiting for me. Time out while I finish reading my mail-

Back again . . . Say, Dad, that surely is a swell letter. Thanks 1,000,000. And the clippings of those fellows, I really enjoy reading about them.

* "It is a crime." Bob was referring to the damage done on one infamous night during the Blitz. On December 29, 1940, around 100,000 bombs fell on London in just a few hours, causing a firestorm across most of the city's square mile up to Islington, later called the Second Great Fire of London.

** Shortly before Noël Coward wrote *Blithe Spirit*, London suffered heavy bombing by the German Luftwaffe, leaving large parts of the city in rubble, including Coward's own apartment. Coward retreated with a friend to Wales to write, hoping to create a play that might provide a few hours of laughter for his compatriots in London and brighten their gloomy days. Apparently, Coward's "light touch on serious matters" did just that for its London audiences. The *Blithe Spirit* ran for almost two thousand performances, setting a record that would not be broken for years on any London stage.

The weather here is warm and nice lately. I'm almost at the ⅓ mark . . . not bad, eh? Things look swell. I should be home for Xmas!

Until I can write soon again,
All my love, Bob

After that brief respite in London, it was back to the war for Bob and the crew. They'd fly six missions to finish up July, five of them to heavily defended targets in Germany. Then with the stress of combat beginning to weigh heavily on them, they would fly another six big combat missions in August. Up next: seventy years later, three of those August missions still stuck out in Bob's mind.

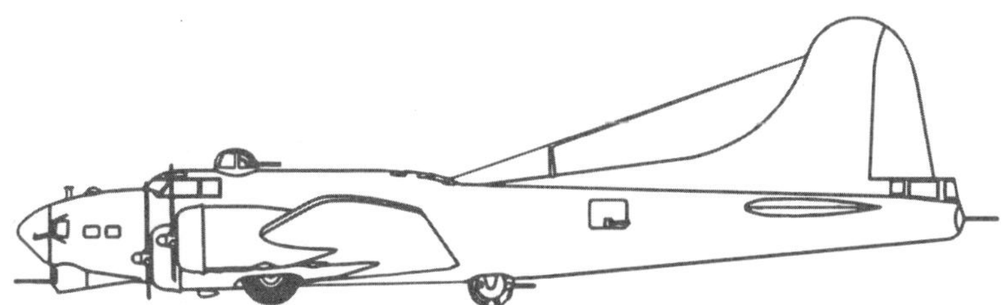

CHAPTER 7
LIFE ON THE BASE AND THREE MISSIONS TO REMEMBER

Mission 15	August 8	Cauvicourt, France	42-40007	"Honey"
Mission 16	August 11	Brest, France	42-97882	unnamed B-17
Mission 17	August 13	Rouen, France	bomber number unknown	
Mission 18	August 25	Neubrandenburg, Germany	42-40007	"Honey"
Mission 19	August 27	Berlin, Germany	44-6095	"Fort Worth Gal"
Mission 20	August 30	Kiel, Germany	42-39997	"Frenchy's Folly"

While researching this book, I filled two notebooks with anecdotes and transcripts of my conversations with Bob Harper. I soon realized that I was gathering some interesting material that wouldn't necessarily fit into the flow of this narrative, and that perhaps the best solution would be to insert a chapter that was a bit more random with some questions and answers. This is that chapter.

During one interview with Bob, I asked him about the inevitable comparison between the two big four-engine bombers used by the 8th Air Force in the European theater of operations: the B-24 Liberator and the B-17 Flying Fortress. During the war, the AAF accepted a total of 12,692 B-17s and 18,190 B-24s. In August 1944, the Army held an inventory of 4,574 B-17s, most of them stationed with the 8th AF in England. While researching the book, I visited an airshow in Oregon and climbed on board both vintage model bombers for a firsthand look. To my 6'2" frame, the B-24 seemed much roomier than the B-17. On the other hand, during the war, the B-24 had been nicknamed the Flying Coffin. So I telephoned Bob and put the question to him: "In your opinion, which was the better aircraft?":

> I never stepped on board a B-24 Liberator. Not once. The two different bombers were always stationed at their own specific bases, to my knowledge. Our B-17 crews were specifically trained to operate the Fortress. I suppose a gunner might have been able to switch over to the other bomber without too many problems, but I doubt the pilots, bombardiers, or navigators could have. At least not without some retraining. Occasionally a damaged B-17 or B-24 seeking the nearest

airfield might limp into a base that serviced only the other bomber and take a ribbing, of course. You know? *Are you guys lost? Any port in a storm?* But I do remember a few conversations, probably from pubs in London, and the crews of both bombers were fiercely loyal to their own plane.

Being prejudiced here, of course, I think the crews of the B-17s felt that we were better off on a B-17 than we would be on a B-24. There were a few times when Joe, our pilot, or another crew member would spot fighters that might be waiting for us, about to attack. And of course, the intercom would light up, tracking them from our different positions . . . and someone might wisecrack, "Hey, where are those B-24s when we need them?" Meaning, of course, the German fighter planes would go after the B-24s first and spare us . . . because the B-24s were an easier target. The B-24 crews probably said the same thing about B-17s. . . . But when you look at the famous pictures of badly damaged B-17s somehow making their way back to base, bringing back their crews alive . . . well, that may be your answer right there.

I asked Bob what life was like when he settled into Ridgewell after that first month of intense combat. Over seventy years had passed by, but he still had some clear memories to share of his early days on the base:

Let me give you a few impressions of our base. The 381st Bomb Group consisted of four separate squadrons: the 532nd, 533rd, 534th, and 535th, and though we occasionally might borrow a plane from one another, we were pretty distinct entities, with our own squadron commanders leading us. Ridgewell was a big base (covering over 600 acres), and the planes from each squadron were separated into groups and parked on what they called hardstands, which were stretched out along the perimeter, far apart from each other.

The base was isolated, located in the pretty English countryside. Between missions there was nothing much to do that summer (1944) except eat and sleep, read books and write letters, play cards, and chess. . . . Letters were important, very important, and mail call was always a big deal. Sometimes there would be a delay, and the letters would pile up. Then a pile would come in and guys might go off by themselves for an hour or two, reading and rereading them. Remember, there were no telephones. Of course, some guys didn't get much mail either. I was lucky; I got my share and tried to write home often.

So, as I said, nothing much to do, unless you could get a pass and head to London or Cambridge. Our crew had grown pretty close while training back in Florida and Georgia. We had hit the beaches there a few times, all of us together. Once we were in England, it wasn't long before I was hanging out with three of our officers: our pilot, Joe Pearce; bombardier, Gene Weisser; and navigator, Mort Yolofsky. I know that there was a lot of separation between the non-coms and the officers on some of the crews, but not on ours. I actually became good friends with mine. I think that goes to the leadership of our pilot, Joe Pearce. He was a great pilot and had everyone's respect. But he wasn't a stiff marionette, and he treated everyone the same. Joe called me "Shorty," and it wasn't an insult back then. A lot of ball turret gunners had that nickname, just a physical fact. This will come as a surprise to a lot of ex-soldiers, but off base, Lieutenants Pearce, Weisser, and Yolofsky were just Joe, Gene, and Mort to me unless we were in the presence of officers or men outside our crew.

One of our pastimes that summer was to bicycle in the beautiful countryside around Ridgewell. Mort, Gene, Joe, and I had bikes or could easily borrow them. That year, July and August had nice weather, and the four of us would jump on those bicycles and head out for a long ride if we didn't have a mission or a training session, sometimes stopping at a pub for a quick lunch and a beer. Focusing on that green English countryside, farms, and gardens helped me to relax. We had some good laughs along the way. And there were those wonderful English flower gardens everywhere. . . . No doubt the exercise helped me to sleep at night as well, given what we were going through some days when we were flying. That countryside was just lovely, and a good break when we could catch one.

On another occasion, I asked Bob if he had gotten to know the maintenance crews that serviced his B-17s. He gave it a long thought before he answered:

Well, not really; just a friendly hello if they were out there when we arrived in the morning. I flew on quite a few planes, and when their ground crews were finishing up, our work was just beginning. Each plane (or hardstand) had its own maintenance crew, usually four or five guys and a crew chief. Sometimes even more men if a big job was underway. You know, I flew on quite a few different B-17s (fourteen), and every one of them had a ground crew who did a wonderful job.

After we got back from one mission where the flak was just murder, our ground crew were waiting for us; they had heard that we'd run into some trouble and our squadron had been hit bad, and they were just sweating it out for us, waiting there. After we taxied to the hardstand, our pilot, Joe Pearce, walked around the bomber, taking the time to inspect the flak damage with the crew chief. The chief told us, and I'll never forget this number, that there were 238 holes from the radio room to the tail. 238! Somehow, we made it back. Not one of my crew was hit that day, but parts of the plane looked like Swiss cheese . . . and a piece of flak was stuck in the turret door as well. If I remember correctly, we were back up in that same B-17 just a few days later.

The B-17G that we flew on wasn't the first version of the B-17, and I read after the war that they made something like three hundred changes to her while she was in service, just updating her from the previous F model and improving her along the way. . . . And these maintenance crews had to keep them flying and deal with all the little modifications. So, it wasn't just patching the holes in the skin, and it seemed like that at least a third of our missions we came back with at least a few. They also had to maintain the oxygen systems, and the electronics, hydraulics, and work on those four monster Wright Cyclone supercharged engines. Sometimes I think those guys lived full-time at the hardstand and in the repair hangars trying to keep the planes operational. They were really part of our crew, and I don't know how much credit they ever got, working under pressure like they did and knowing they had to get it right for us, sometimes working under lights through the night in about as rotten weather as you could imagine, fueling them up, loading them with bombs and ammo . . . to get them ready for an early-morning mission.

One day I put this question to Bob: "I've seen the pictures of a B-17 crew bundled up and posing in their bulky flight suits. Just how cold were you up there?":

Yes, good question. [Bob laughed] The cold was always an issue for the crew. Our average altitude when headed for a mission, as I recall, was about 22,000 to 25,000 feet. We wanted to get as high as possible, because that made the German antiaircraft guns less effective. Starting at about 18,000 feet, the temperature ranged from 40 to 60 degrees below zero. I guess the previous year, before we got to Ridgewell, quite a few men came back from missions badly frostbit. So we were all warned that cold would be one of our constant hazards, and about every three or four minutes during a mission there was a radio check by the copilot, so they knew that no one had passed out due to oxygen freezing on the way to our mask—this was true as well when we took flak or ran into fighters; the pilots would want to make sure an oxygen line hadn't been shot out.

By the time we got into combat, the B-17 model G had sliding windows on the waist guns, but there was plenty of places where the air could get in. If you think about it, the fuselage was just a thin metal sheet with no insulation. So, they insulated us instead. [Bob laughed again]

To overcome the cold, the Army issued us special equipment. My flying suit consisted of three layers: First came socks and long underwear and a light woolen shirt. The next layer was cloth pants and jacket lining with electric heaters running through it that could be plugged in like an electric sleeping blanket. Over that was a third layer, with insulated flying pants and fleece-lined jacket. I wore silk gloves under fur-lined gloves and insulated flying boots over wired, felt boots. The idea was that the heated suit, gloves, and boot linings would keep your body warm, while the heavy outer layer kept that heat in. When I climbed down into the ball turret, I would plug the electric suit in. It had a rheostat, but I didn't turn it on until we started really gaining altitude. In the summer I would wait until we were airborne before putting on the outer layer. We were all concerned about sweating and soaking our inner layers. It was hard to get the timing just right.

My own gun turret leaked air like a sieve. Imagine going about 180 mph in an unheated car with the window half open on a cold winter's day.

The rubber oxygen mask that I wore was about as uncomfortable a thing that you could imagine. The air in the ball turret would easily be −50 Fahrenheit. So, as you breathed in and out, the warm air from your lungs heated the rubber, and the condensation on the outside would quickly form a sheet of ice, which you kept having to break away. It became second nature, but at the end of the mission your face could get pretty raw.

Early in our talks, I read part of a letter from June 29, 1944, out loud to Bob; he had sent it home after his first week at Ridgewell, remarking on the food:

> I can't get over the wonderful chow we have here. My gosh, it's just not army food! We have our own chow hall (combat crews). Every morning we either have fresh fried eggs or hot cakes (delicious) along with the daily choices of cereals, bacon, coffee, cocoa, and fruit. Just for example, here's lunch today; Pork chops, mashed potatoes, and gravy, creamed corn, sliced lettuce salad, carrots,—the dessert was cake with sauce over it.
>
> Right now I'm in the library of our Red Cross Aero club. Nothing elaborate, but nice. These little things help out all. We have a record machine in the lounge, and the ladies have swell snacks prepared for us every night in the snack bar.

Bob laughed:

> It's true, I know a lot of guys didn't, but I always liked Army food, especially at Ridgewell. It helped with the morale for sure. By the time I got to Ridgewell, we had invaded the continent, and our soldiers were slugging it out with the Nazis on the ground under tough, tough conditions. We read the service magazines, and they told the story pretty graphically. So, I was always grateful to have a bunk at night, even if our Nissen hut was freezing that winter and we had to slog through the mud to get a barely lukewarm shower or to the mess hall. I appreciated that the boys on the ground were grinding it out in their dugouts, just holes in the mud, living off cold food.
>
> On the other hand, climbing into the B-17 wasn't getting any easier for any of us with each passing mission. Some of the things we were seeing and going through, you could close your eyes and relive them back at the base . . . or dream about them at night. . . . And then those bombing runs into those fields of flak, where you could do nothing . . . it seemed like an awful lot of close calls. With each mission it was getting harder to climb back on board.

In a short journal written after the war, Bob wrote about some of his missions. I telephoned him one day and asked him to expand on those memories. We had discussed this a few weeks prior, so he was ready to talk about them:

It happened long ago, so to be perfectly honest, it is easy now to get them tangled up. But I thought about what you said, and I guess there were some missions I will always remember; these are three that stick out in my mind; as you mentioned, I wrote about them in that journal:

Zwickau, Germany: The mission of the 8th Air Force was not to hurt or kill civilians, it was to damage and destroy the war machine of the Germans—the oil refineries, the bridges (we hit a lot of bridges), the factories that made aircraft, tanks, ball bearings; those were our main targets. I'm sure what we did certainly shortened the war, because we really crippled their industry.

But there was kind of a sad mission that we flew that fall when the strategy of the 8th Air Force called for what they said was a "morale mission," an attempt to break the spirit of the German people and shorten the war. So that day, instead of our usual industrial or military targets, all of the 8th AF (some 1,200 bombers at that time) bombed small cities, towns, and villages where people would stand out in the streets and watch us fly over day after day. It was a tough mission to fly, but I guess that's just part of that bloody war. For years I struggled with the memory of that day. [*Author's note*: This was probably the mission to Zwickau in October, a small, picturesque city of 80,000 that had been already mostly demolished by Allied bombing by the fall of 1944 but still had the remnants of a motor vehicle factory and what was left of an airport.]

Peenemunde, Germany: On the other hand, there was one long, dangerous mission I clearly remember, when I returned back to base feeling really good. Really good. We flew to Peenemunde that day to hit the site of the German rocket programs (August 25, Neubrandenburg, Germany). That was a real enterprising mission. That morning, we went out and half of that bomb-bay was filled with a big black plastic, auxiliary gas tank. So, we knew we had a long one; it turned out to be more than eleven hours.

We flew up over the North Sea and down over Kiel. Then we hit Neubrandenburg pretty hard. I had seen the damage to London up close from those German rockets and bombs, those rows of houses and apartment buildings leveled, the underground still full of civilians at night. Well, it was really satisfying because we flattened Peenemunde. Then we flew back over the North Sea. In the briefing that morning, they said that if you ditched in the North Sea, you could live in that water only a couple of minutes or so, because it was so cold. But it was also the safest route back, and everything worked out fine. We had been warned it was a very dangerous mission, but it went just fine. The 8th Air Force did a good job that day!

Kiel, Germany: Kiel was another long, memorable mission (August 30, 1944). We hit the submarine pens there. That was another target that took a lot of work because the weather there and back was terrible, and we had to bomb using PFF (Pathfinder radio location system). There was moderate flak over the target, but I guess it was a case of "if we can't see you, then you can't see us." Probably not true, but we used to tell ourselves that, because those long white contrails that we put up when the skies were clear were really like arrows pointing right at us for those German flak gunners waiting below.

Of course, by the time we got over there, the summer of '44, the German flak batteries were getting better and better, more numerous and more sophisticated. I had a computerized gunsight on my .50 machine guns, and though we didn't want to think about it, we knew that the flak guns had their own sophisticated aiming systems. Some of our missions included throwing out aluminum chaff to confuse their radars. But the German antiaircraft emplacements were getting bigger and better, and we were feeling the results. And the problem for our crews was that we couldn't shoot back; you had to sit there and take it. . . . You could only hope that the bombs that you were dropping might take out a few guns and make it easier for the next guy . . . or for you the next day . . . because sometimes I remember having to go back to the same target more than once.

But hitting those submarine pens that day. As teenagers we all heard many stories of the German Wolf Packs in the Atlantic, attacking British merchant convoys and unarmed ships, and it had some sort of effect on me. Those graphic stories of ships going down in the cold Atlantic waters were in all the newspapers. So, it was one thing to go out on those big raids bombing German cities and their manufacturing plants, you know? Oil, ball bearings, airplane engines, bridges. That was important work. But the idea of going after their submarines made that mission to Kiel a little different, a lot like when we went after the rocket launchers. Sort of like we were really engaging the actual enemy.

After the war was over and I went back to St. Louis, I was able to meet up with Gene Fears, my best friend from childhood and from high school tennis-playing days. Gene was a fine tennis player, probably one of the best tennis players in St. Louis at the time, though he was still just a teenager. About the time I was drafted, Gene went into the merchant marine, and he was out on those seas during the war, at risk from those German subs. Of course, when we renewed our acquaintance and our friendship after the war, Gene told me that he had sailed around the world four or five times. He had wonderful stories to tell about convoys and what life was like on those dangerous seas. But to answer your question, I don't recall if I ever told him about that long mission to take out those submarine pens.

THE FINAL FLIGHT OF B-17 44-6995, "FORT WORTH GAL"

In researching Bob's thirty-five missions, I found that some histories of the planes that Bob crewed on were much better documented than others. If a plane had been given a catchy name, it seemed like there would be more references to it than a plane that went unnamed and could be identified only by its number. As a way of honoring a few of the other heroic 381st bomber crews, men whose stories have mostly gone untold, I decided to spend a moment with the "Fort Worth Gal," one of the fourteen B-17s that Bob flew on, in addition to dedicating a chapter to his favorite Flying Fortress, "Honey."

On August 27, 1944, Bob flew on the "Fort Worth Gal" to Berlin, and though it was a long mission, and the flak was heavy over the target, they made it back unscathed. But the "Fort Worth Gal's" luck was running out, and just three days later a different crew took the "Fort Worth Gal" to Keil, Germany, and were badly shot up. Here is the 381st mission report illustrating how the brave teamwork of Lt. Rolin's crew kept the "Fort Worth Gal" from going down that day:

> Working severed propeller and throttle control cables with his hands in the cramped nose compartment of "Fort Worth Gal," a 533rd ship, top turret gunner S/Sgt. Nile E. Greathouse became an unofficial "third pilot" on today's mission to Kiel. During the bombing run over the German port city, "Fort Worth Gal" was struck by a vicious burst of flak which severed the throttle and prop control cables, frayed the aileron cables, and knocked out the oxygen system used by the pilot, navigator, and engineer.

> The bomber fell out of formation and dropped 6,000 feet before the pilot, 1Lt. Mitchell A. Rolin, could pull it back to level flight. Throttles gone, the pilot had no means of regulating speed until Sgt Greathouse left his turret and crawled into the nose beneath the co-pilot's seat to work the snapped cables with his hands. Coached by the pilot over the interphone, the top turret gunner handled the throttle controls perfectly and the bomber crawled back to England at 130 mph. "To show you the job Greathouse did, though," Lt. Rolin said later, "We still beat the rest of the formation home."

On September 10, after an extensive week of repair work, the "Fort Worth Gal" went out on another mission. It would be her last. The event was witnessed by nearby B-17 crews and recorded during the intelligence debriefings that took place later that day, when the surviving bombers returned to base.

> I, Sgt. Robert E. Tyler, was acting as waist gunner in Aircraft No. 43-37561, 533rd Squadron, which was flying in the left-wing position in the same flight with Lt. Germano's Aircraft ("Fort Worth Gal"), on the 10th of September 1944, when I saw Lt. Germano peel out of formation. He banked off to the right at 90° from the formation, then he made another 180° turn and flew directly across the back of our formation. He flew along until he was out of my sight. Three engines were smoking when I last saw him.

Eight crew members of the "Fort Worth Gal" parachuted to safety and became POWs. The ninth, tail gunner Sgt. Harry Siders, was discovered by villagers, hanging from a tree by his parachute, already dead from bullet wounds.

The "Fort Worth Gal" was one of 346 bombers assigned to the 381st Bomb Group during the war. Of those 346 bombers, 141 would be lost, a 41 percent attrition rate. Of the fourteen B-17s that Bob crewed on, eight would also be either shot down or crash-land. Bob's favorite B-17, "Honey," would figure prominently on the list of famous 381st B-17s before her own demise.

Up next is "Honey's" story.

CHAPTER 8
"HONEY'S" EIGHTY-SEVEN COMBAT MISSIONS AND THE 365 MEN WHO CREWED HER

Bob Harper:

> Whenever I thought back to the war, and some time passed before I allowed myself to think much about those days, "Honey" was the only B-17 that I really remembered well. When we began flying on the "Honey," midway through our first month of combat, our crew was still the same one that I had trained with back in Florida.
>
> Of course, there is not much more I can say about our first mission on "Honey," the day that "Fleming" made a run for it. But we flew the "Honey" pretty steadily afterwards, maybe six or seven times. . . . A few of those missions were milk runs, but some of them were long, tough ones into Germany: Schweinfurt, Merseburg, and Munich. Heavily defended targets, and we were blasted by flak and once or twice we ran into fighters. And yet, each time the "Honey" delivered us safely home to Ridgewell . . . patched up, she was ready to go again in a couple of days. It felt like the "Honey" would be our lucky charm, and there wasn't any of us on the crew that doubted by then that we might need one.
>
> Then we were given a two-day pass, and when we returned from London, we heard that she had gone out with another crew and been shot down (September 12). A few of the guys had left personal items on "Honey." I remember that sinking feeling to this day. So much for luck . . . I don't know why we were so surprised. We felt bad for the missing crew, of course. And then we felt that perhaps we had dodged a bullet. Another bullet . . . after that, I stopped caring what plane I was on. I just wanted to get my missions done and get back home.

After reading Bob's journal and interviewing him at length, I began searching for more clues about "Honey's" fate. It wasn't too long before I discovered that "Honey" wasn't shot down that day when she hadn't returned to base but had landed outside Paris. My search also turned up the crew lists for each of "Honey's" eighty-seven combat missions, a rare stroke of luck for a researcher (thanks to Chris Tennet of the 381st Memorial Group). Armed with that list, I was able to delve more deeply into "Honey's" amazing combat history. I thought by selecting a few missions here, we would pay tribute to the men who crewed the "Honey," all 365 of them!

Mission 1

B-17 42-0007, known as "Honey," began her service with the 381st Bomber Group, 533rd Squadron, on January 29, 1944. Crewed by the pilot, 2Lt. Bob Deering, and his nine-man crew, the "Honey" took a long trip to Frankfurt, Germany. Her maiden mission was documented in the 381st BG combat diary:

> Formation after formation of Fortresses thundered over Frankfurt today, dropping tons of explosives on the important industrial city through a heavy overcast. Squadron commander, Maj. George Shackley, flew in the lead ship "Sweet and Lovely," ahead of 33 aircraft, eight supplied by the 533rd. "The sky was black behind us after we passed over Frankfurt," he said, "and the formations behind us must have caught hell." He estimated about 125 fighters were defending Frankfurt.

On the following day, Lt. Deering and most of the "Honey's" inaugural crew were assigned to a different B-17, the "Wolverine." Of the thirty-one bombers that the 381st contributed to that raid on Braunschweig, Germany, the "Wolverine," "Martha the II," and "Chap's Flying Circus" didn't make it back. Badly crippled from continued fighter attacks, the "Wolverine" exploded, its remains landing near a small German village. Lt. Deering and seven of the crew were killed. One crew member managed to parachute to safety and became a POW. It was Deering's seventh mission.

Mission 20

Despite the bad fortune for the "Honey's" inaugural crew, all ran smoothly for the men flying on her over the next two months. Despite running into the heavy flak and enemy fighters that were typical during those late-winter raids of 1944, "Honey's" crews managed their next eighteen missions without casualties. On March 29, the "Honey" flew to Braunschweig, Germany, where most of her inaugural crew had perished aboard the "Wolverine."

In the 1930s, Braunschweig was known as one of the most beautiful medieval cities in Europe, with over a thousand ancient timber-framed dwellings. But Braunschweig was also the first German city to embrace Hitler, granting him German citizenship in 1932, enabling him to run for president. As a Nazi political stronghold and the garrison city of the 31st Infantry Division, Braunschweig would be the subject of forty-two Allied bombings and 90 percent leveled by the end of the war. When "Honey" set out for Braunschweig that morning, piloted by Lt. Milton Tarr, sitting in the copilot's seat was a guest, Maj. Charles Halsey, the 535th Squadron's commanding officer. An entry from flight surgeon Maj. Gallaird's diary tells the story of "Honey's" close call and how the rugged construction of the B-17 saved the crew that day:

> March 29, 1944. Fortresses of the 381st caught their first glimpse of the Luftwaffe in action in many days when an estimated 150 German fighters made a concerted attack on the bomber formation as it swept over Brunswick today [for some reason, probably making it easier to pronounce, the 8th AF always referred to Braunschweig as Brunswick]. . . . Attacking enemy fighters were immediately engaged by escorting allied fighters in violent dogfights after the single pass at the B-17s.
>
> Although preliminary reports show only two men wounded, several of the ships returned to base with heavy battle damage. One of the hardest hit was the 533rd's, "Honey." Attacking fighters knocked out "Honey's" right inboard engine and tore up the radio room floor with 20 mm cannon shells. No one aboard was injured, and although the pilot was forced to drop behind the formation, the ship came safely home. Shortly after the engine went dead, a second shell exploded in the flooring directly under the radioman, Sgt. Smith, knocking him to the floor. Ground crewmen later traced the course of the shell from its entrance through the right wing, through the flooring to the explosion that destroyed all Sgt. Smith's radio equipment, blew up an oxygen bottle behind him, and tore a large hole in the wall of his compartment. Apart from a bruised elbow Sgt. Smith was unhurt.

The trip to Braunschweig put "Honey" out of commission for three weeks while extensive repairs were made. On April 22, "Honey" would be back in action and flying two or three missions a week. Ten weeks and twenty-three combat missions later, "Honey" was once again mentioned in the flight surgeon's 242nd medical diary (July 7). This time the heroism of her crew managed to create their own luck and bring the bomber safely back to base:

Mission 42

July 7, 1944:

> When Lt. Lee V Wilson's 533rd fortress, "Honey," pulled out of a 2,000-foot plunge, necessitated to avoid colliding with another bomber during the return trip from France yesterday, four bombs were ripped from their shackles and slammed into the bomb bay door. Six more swung loosely from badly weakened attachments. Armorer-tail gunner SSgt. Clyde C. Crain crawled forward to the bay, saw the predicament, and realized the four, floored bombs might explode under the slightest jar at any moment. Nevertheless, he began safe-tying the remaining bombs in their shackles, while Wilson headed for the channel to salvo the deadly load. [*Author's note*: The bombs were already "safe-tied" when loaded on board, and the "safe-tie" wire was removed only once the B-17 was safely in flight, thus arming the bomb. When it was determined for any reason that the bombs were not going to be used, the in-flight crew could reinsert the wires again, safe-tying them.]
>
> As he was working without a parachute, a loose bomb knocked Crain down into the bay among the live explosives. He climbed back and, assisted by bombardier 2Lt. Richard E Kennedy, continued with the safe-tying. Honey made it to the channel [English Channel], where her flight engineer, top-turret gunner Sgt. George N. Myers, began lowering the bomb bay doors under the guidance from the two men in the Bay. Not daring to jolt the loose bombs, Meyers eased the hand crank a few threads at a time until, in a tight cluster, they slipped clear and downward to the water. Then Crain and Kennedy released the remaining explosives singly and by hand until the bay was clear. Wilson then turned "Honey" for home, landing safely more than an hour behind the rest of the formation.

Mission 47

A week later the Pearce crew, with Bob Harper aboard, began their stint with "Honey," with a mission to Augsburg on July 16 (marked by Sgt. Fleming's exit). They would fly "Honey" on missions to Schweinfurt, St. Lô, Merseburg (twice), Cauvicourt, and finally, on August 25, to Neubrandenburg. Two weeks later, while Bob and his crewmates were in London, the "Honey" would fail to return from her sixty-fifth mission, and Bob would assume she had been lost. Clear details of "Honey's" actual fate that day wouldn't emerge until the 242nd Medical Attachments diary was eventually published after the war.

Mission 65

On September 12, "Honey" failed to return to base. Her fate was meticulously recorded by two entries in the 242nd medical diary:

> September 12, 1944: 37 aircraft from this command took off at 07.30 hrs. for the target at Brux-on-Most, Czechoslovakia. The lead group, led by Col Hall, attacked the primary target, blind and unobserved, and the high and low groups attacked targets of opportunity. There was some enemy fighter activity but not many were seen. There was considerable battle damage to our aircraft, caused by flak. One of our aircraft has not reported in (Piloted by Lt. McMullen, 533rd, 42-40007, "Honey"), but it is thought he landed in France with one crewman KIA and two cases of frostbite.

September 15, 1944

Recently missing 533rd pilot (Lt. Donald P. McMullen), with his crew, was flying with an entirely new crew on the mission to Czechoslovakia, which was designated more to draw enemy fighters than for any particular bombing mission.

His ship, a B-17G called "Honey," had been flying at 22,000 feet for some two and a half hours. Oxygen checks were being made every fifteen minutes. The radio operator's microphone was not working, and he had been relaying his oxygen checks to the waist gunner. The radioman answered his oxygen check before the IP and then turned around to throw out chaff. He failed to answer his oxygen check fifteen minutes later.

The waist gunner, Sgt. Meyers J. Barker, was asked to investigate, and when he failed to report in, the ball turret man, Sgt. Lydell A. Hayes, was ordered to investigate. When in another five minutes neither of these men reported, the engineer went back to investigate and found all three men unconscious. The radioman, Sgt. Joseph J. Charkowski, was lying on the floor by the outlet into which he throws the chaff, his mask was off, and the face end was disconnected from the oxygen outlet.

The engineer put his mask on Charkowski's face, connected the hose, and turned on the emergency oxygen supply, and the radioman made an immediate recovery and after a short rest period was able to resume his duties as a radio operator. He received a frostbite of the left side of face and cheek, moderate severity.

Waist gunner Hayes was lying at the entrance to the radio operator's entrance, and his mask was off his face and completely disconnected from the G-1 oxygen bottle, which was lying beside him. He had taken off his right glove and his hand was frostbitten. The engineer placed his mask on Hayes's face and connected him to the oxygen outlet, and he made a full recovery and was placed in the radio room under protective covers. The engineer's own bottle was running low about this time, and he went back and got the tail gunner to help him, and the bombardier came back later.

He found the ball turret gunner lying unconscious under the right waist gun; his mask was off his face and disconnected and full of frozen vomitus. It was disconnected from a full G-1 walk-around bottle lying beside him. A mask was placed on this man's face, emergency oxygen was given, and then artificial respiration, which was continued for approximately one and a half hours on the ship and later on the ground, without signs of life returning.

The radio man did not remember what happened after he started to throw out chaff (aluminum strips that were intended to confuse enemy radar); the waist gunner did not remember what happened after he started forward with the walk-around bottle. The ship left the formation about ten minutes after the discovery of the unconscious men and dove 1,700 feet per minute at 250 mph to 4,000 feet, then returned over the greater part of Germany, including the Siegfried Line, at this altitude without enemy interference. They landed at a fighter airfield inside France, where the medical officer, after giving artificial respiration to the ball turret gunner, pronounced him dead and recommended that they take these men to another airfield near Paris, which was done.

The radio operator had a moderately severe frostbite on the side of his face, and the waist gunner had severe frostbite of the right hand. It is estimated that the radioman was unconscious for more than twenty-five minutes, and the waist gunner for not more than ten, and no more than fifteen to twenty minutes elapsed before oxygen and artificial respiration was given to the ball turret gunner. The latter had been drinking heavily the night before and had had not more than an hour's sleep prior to the mission.

The cause of the three anoxic incidents was personnel failure. All masks and ship connections had been checked just a few days prior to the mission by the equipment officer. They all were equipped with the new M-45 modification with the quick disconnect, which makes it virtually impossible for the connections to come apart if inserted at all. The oxygen system of the plane was checked after it landed at this base, and was found satisfactory.

The engineer on this ship, who had the same training as the other crewmen, was questioned and appeared to have adequate training and possessed an adequate knowledge of oxygen equipment and its use.

Mission 87

"Honey" continued to fly combat missions that autumn, almost all of them deep into German territory. Repaired and patched up, she would be sent out again and again, occasionally with new crews adding to the growing list of her flight alumni. When "Honey" failed to return from mission 65, her copilot that day was Lt. Henry Riza. As fate would have it, six weeks later (on November 25), Lt. Riza would also be on board "Honey," this time serving as pilot. This bombing run to heavily defended Merseburg would be "Honey's" final one. Years after the war ended, the radio operator aboard the "Honey" that day, Sgt. Bob Tyler, provided his family with a firsthand account of that day:

> We were on a high-altitude bombing mission deep inside Germany, and the plane ("Honey") that we had was pretty patched up and tired. It was having trouble reaching the altitude we needed, and we lost an engine. This in itself was not all that bad, except we could not keep up with the rest of the squadron and had to drop back on our own. Soon we lost another engine and found ourselves trying to find our way across Germany alone. Out of nowhere one of our fighter escorts appeared and flew with us until his fuel level forced him to leave.
>
> We soon lost a third engine, which meant we were flying with one, and that was not good. We did not know where we were and were slowly coming down. Our pilot said that we should consider jumping, but we knew that meant being taken prisoner or worse. We decided to stay with the plane. By this time, we were so low we could see the ground fighting going on below us. The pilot had very little control at this point. We came down in a field with our wheels up; no one got a scratch. We were in Belgium, not too far from Brussels. It took us a week to get back to England and our base. To this day I do not know why we had not been reported as MIA, but I am glad that they had waited.

WARTIME SECRECY AND THE "HONEY"

It's interesting to reflect on why Bob's crew never discovered "Honey's" real fate. When the airfields were first constructed for the incoming American 8th Air Force, England was subject to aerial bombardment by the German

Luftwaffe and by the occasional V-1 rockets, also known as "buzz bombs." With bitter lessons learned from the devastating Japanese airstrikes on air bases in Hawaii and the Pacific still fresh in American minds, each of the 8th Air Force's airfields was designed so that their precious bombers were spread out over as much available farmland as possible to minimize the potential damage to planes, facilities, and ammo dumps should the Germans strike the field. Bob's base at Ridgewell, for instance, had fifty-six hardstands for the B-17s scattered around the perimeter of its 600-acre facility.

The noncommissioned officers (sergeants) also led a somewhat insular life, with two crews of five or six men to a small Nissen hut. Though they messed in the same mess hall, these men usually stayed with their own crews. On base, wartime information was fragmented and compartmentalized for security, especially considering that each week, bomber crews would bail out over enemy territory and be subject to capture and interrogation by the Germans. Airmen were given the minimum amount of information that they needed to know, and were constantly advised not to share any mission information with those back home. Bob didn't learn of "Honey's" survival back in September, so of course he also didn't know of her second forced landing in Belgium:

> Ridgewell was a big base with four different squadrons, and it wasn't in the nature of the job that we were specifically informed of individual aircraft losses. We basically stuck to our barracks and ate at the same table at the mess. We really didn't interact with a lot of guys outside of our crew and the other crew of noncoms in our Nissen hut. There were good reasons for that, of course; you just didn't want to get close to the other guys. Depending on how many missions they had left, or their luck, they could be gone the next day. Of course, maybe some of the other crews were different. There was a baseball field and the like. But that was us. We pretty much stuck to ourselves.
>
> We also got a lot less information about what was happening than you might imagine. We rarely knew the names of the other planes that were flying in our formation on any given mission unless they were sitting on our wing. Our officers of course got better information; they knew which other planes and pilots from our squadron were going up with us, they were in that briefing room with them, they saw the formation diagrams, but it wasn't discussed much among the officers either.

> Three of the officers on our crew became good friends of mine, but we rarely talked about the war when we had a chance to get away from it. . . . If we got a two- or three-day pass, I would head off for London or Cambridge with Studebaker and our pilot, navigator, and bombardier . . . Joe, Gene, and Mort. So, this is a long way round of saying it, but I never did get the details on the Honey after she went missing on September 12th . . . I don't think any of us heard that she had survived another two months. Probably the only way that we would have found out is if we flew on her . . . or she was sitting on our wing. But that didn't happen.

After she force-landed for the second time, "Honey" spent December 1944 sitting on her belly "wheels up" in a field in Belgium. Picked apart by the local civilians, her gas tanks were emptied of valuable fuel; her guns, radios, and navigational equipment were reclaimed and salvaged by the 8th Air Force. A shell of herself, local townspeople began using "Honey" as a backdrop for photographs.

JUST HOW WELL DID "HONEY" MEASURE UP TO OTHER B-17S?

After spending a bit of time investigating "Honey," a question occurred to me: Was the service and longevity of "Honey" a typical one for a B-17?

For starters, in addition to "Honey" there were 346 B-17s assigned to the 381st Bomber Group during the war. Of those, 143 (roughly 40 percent) were lost in combat and accidents. Several of those B-17s were downed on their very first missions, while three of them managed to complete over a hundred missions and survive the war: the "Stage Door Canteen," 116 missions; "Rotherhithe's Revenge" and the "Avengress II," 102 missions each.

For a different perspective, I traced the "Honey's" pilot histories. Of the forty-two different men who piloted "Honey," four were killed in action while commanding other B-17s, one died in a crash while training a new crew, one was captured by the Germans and became a POW, and, finally, one was interned in Switzerland when his B-17 force-landed there. A similar percentage of "Honey's" other crew members were lost aboard other B-17s.

I soon gave up hope for any real definitive analysis, wartime records being what they are, but did come to this conclusion: typical or not, it turned out that "Honey" was a lucky ship to serve on, losing only two of her 365 crewmen during her eighty-seven combat missions, including Fleming, the man who ran, and Lydell, the ball turret gunner who died of asphyxia.

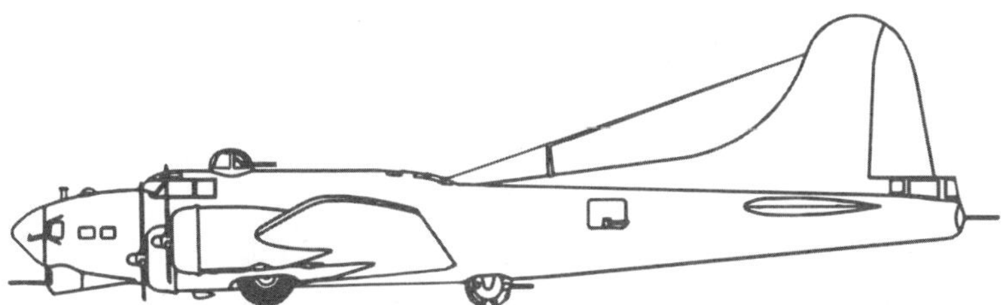

CHAPTER 9
ANOTHER DANGEROUS MISSION TO MERSEBURG AND A VISIT TO THE FLAK HOTEL

Mission 21	September 11	Merseburg	42-31761	"Rotherhithe's Revenge"
Mission 22	September 28	Magdeburg	43-37561	unnamed B-17

Bob Harper:

> It's funny how I dread to fly, but still in all I want to finish up. Well, that's just the way things go.

By all accounts, July and August were tough months for Bob Harper's crew. Bob told me that when September finally rolled around, they were all feeling the strain of combat. Their planes were often hit by flak, on one occasion resulting in more than two hundred holes in the fuselage and wings. Though none of their crew had been wounded, there were too many close calls to list, and they continued to witness other B-17s going down in the far distance and a few much closer.

The Air Force Statistical Report published after the war confirmed Bob's observations: in September 1944, the 8th AF would lose 374 heavy bombers (B-17s and B-24s) in the European theater of operations, making it the third-worst month of the entire war.

Bob and his crew began to wonder out loud about how long their luck might hold. Though they were given two-day passes on a couple of occasions, they all were hopeful of getting away from the war for a promised weeklong break at a flak hotel. Their mood was caught perfectly in this letter home.

> August 31, 1944.
>
> Dear Mom and Dad,
>
> I just picked up two swell letters from Mac our mailman. And after the three-week lull in mail, it seems awfully good or should I say better than usual.

Today was payday and for the first time since I've been over here, I really am going to need this roll of pounds this month. We have a lot to look forward to. First of all, our pass comes up Sunday, and then in about another week we leave for seven days in a wonderful rest home, and from what the fellows here say about it, well, it sounds awfully good.

A beautiful day today, clear, and windy. Already though the breeze and nights are becoming quite chilly. I was surprised to have today off. Happily, so. It's funny how I dread to fly but still in all I want to finish up. Well, that's just the way things go.

Mom, no fooling, your letters get better and better. I enjoy all the news so much. And here I am with not much to say.

Did I mention I received my second oak leaf cluster. I surely enjoy them as I know it means those missions are behind me. Gosh! I can think back to the time when we were only had two or three, just starting. We've come a long way since. 14 to go for me.

Well, after much thought I have a few things I could use. And mom if you could mail this box as soon as possible it can be my X-mas present. I'm positive I won't be here X-mas so there you are. The boys are going home from here as soon as they finish up now. Last week they changed the procedures; you used to have to wait three months after you missions were completed, but no more. So, I have hopes of being home soon.

Old France is really being decontaminated of Germans. Today the boys took Rome and are 30 miles from Belgium and 80 from swastika (Germany). Of course, this will be old news by the time this reaches home. But it surely sounds good, doesn't it?

Mom, I can't tell you how much the Globe and Post funny sections are enjoyed here. It takes me an hour to read a section because I believe I eat up every word on both sides. Next to the funnies, I especially enjoy contract bridge by the Four Aces. And all the short articles. I really enjoy the papers like that more than anything I can think of.

Oh, other things for the box. Pepsodent toothpaste (tube) and some Ingrams shaving cream, Dad. I surely love it, mine is a bit low. Also, about two dozen razor blades or so. My vitamins are also low. And I could use a pair of garters very much. That's really all I can think of, folks. The paper and pictures of you all are about my best present. In my next box please send khaki shirt, four pairs of brown army dress socks, and candy, of course.

Thanks again, Bob

But the promised week of rest and relaxation would have to wait.

On September 11, Bob was shaken awake before dawn. After a quick breakfast, "by mission twenty or so, those fresh eggs no longer held the same charm," they gathered under the belly of a B-17 named "Rotherhithe's Revenge." When pilot Joe Pearce arrived, he gave them the lowdown; they were heading out again for the heavily defended Leuna Oil Works in Merseburg, Germany. Back in July, Bob had been to Merseburg on back-to-back missions, and the ferociously defended target had lived up to its reputation. But in the weeks following their last visit to Merseburg, the slowly retreating German armies had contributed even more flak guns to defend this critical resource, making Merseburg one of the most heavily defended targets in all of Europe. Despite the onslaught from British and American bombers, the Leuna Oil Works were turning out to be particularly resilient. As they climbed aboard their B-17 that morning, they couldn't help remembering what lay ahead.

The Leuna Oil Works had pioneered the process of extracting oil products from lignite (brown coal tar), and the utilization of the byproducts from that process generated Germany's second-largest source of chemicals, many of them used in the production of explosives. Spread out over 3 square miles and staffed by 35,000 production workers, including 10,000 slave laborers, these oil facilities were a huge target that utilized dummy warehouses disguised as factories in an attempt to dilute the bombers' damage. An army of 62,000 flak corps, including 3,200 female Luftwaffe auxiliaries known as *Flakhelferinnen*, 6,000 schoolboys called *Flakhelfer*, and 3,600 Soviet POWs, manned and serviced the antiaircraft guns entrenched in wide rings around the city.

When the Allied bombers managed to hit the oil works, they were quickly rebuilt using both civilian and slave labor. There was even a saying, specifically attributed to the German workers at Leuna:

> *Heute haben wir die Anlagen wieder aufgebaut und morgen kommen die Bomber wieder* (Today we have finished rebuilding the plants and tomorrow the bombers will come again.)

As the Germans retreated before the Russian onslaught on the Eastern Front, they lost their natural oil fields in Ploesti, Hungary, and the synthetic production facilities at Merseburg became even more vital to their war efforts. Donald Miller, in *Masters of the Air*:

> Thus began a protracted duel between the bomber crews and the Luftwaffe pilots, flak directors, and conscript labor forces trying to keep production going. At stake was the tactical mobility of the Wehrmacht and the last hopes for the Luftwaffe to challenge Allied air superiority. At the center of it all was dreaded Leuna. Overall, 6,552 bomber sorties dropped 18,328 tons of bombs on it.
>
> Most flak gunners were deployed in batteries of six to 12 guns. Around Leuna, Speer set up Grossbatterie, each of them equipped with up to 36 guns capable of firing a barrage or box of shells into a prearranged spot.

On September 11, the 8th Air Force headed out for Merseburg and once again paid the price. Flying on "Rotherhithe's Revenge,"* Bob and his crew were among the thirty-seven bombers contributed by the 381st BG to the raid that day:**

> **8th Air Force Mission Report 351**. B-17s were dispatched to hit oil refineries at Merseburg and were subject to both enemy aircraft and heavy flak. One in every 25 of those B-17s were shot down (13 B-17s) and 30% of them returned damaged (108). The toll in airmen were 2 KIA, 21 WIA, and 120 MIA.

Though the "Rotherhithe's Revenge" escaped damage, Bob witnessed the incredible chaos of the battle: bombers going down in the distance, determined German fighters flying headlong through B-17 formations, heavy flak rising to greet them, "so thick it felt that we could land on them." With his third mission to Merseburg behind him, Bob settled back into his Nissen hut to "digest" the experience. A few days later, Bob wrote home. It

* "Rotherhithe's Revenge" was such an unusual name that I searched out its origins and found that it was named for a London community that had suffered heavily in the beginning of the war: From October 1940 to June 1941, the Luftwaffe dropped 1,651 bombs on the Southwark area of London, along with twenty parachute mines. The Bermondsey and Rotherhithe neighborhoods in that area were shattered by that onslaught, with Bermondsey experiencing 395 air raids in the last three months of 1940 alone. In response, stalwart Londoners raised over 800,000 pounds and bought four B-17s, "the Bermondsey Bombers," for the 8th AF to use, hoping they would return the favor to the Germans. Three of those B-17s were stationed at the 381st BG, and one of them, named "Rotherhithe's Revenge," would fly 102 missions, dropping over 300 tons of bombs on Nazi targets.

** Much has been written about Merseburg. One of the best articles that I found is "Twenty Missions in Hell," by Rebecca Grant, which appeared in the April 1, 2007, issue of *Air and Space Forces Magazine*. Grant wrote at length about some of the most notable missions, including November 21, 1944, the day that Bob Harper was shot down.

is the shortest letter that he wrote during the war, and revealed that he had been sharing the growing strain of combat with his father, before thanking him for his morale support.

September 15, 1944

Dear Dad,

That was really a peach of a letter you sent, to say nothing of the wonderful article. I've read it, every word, and it helps my morale quite a bit—especially your underlined "take it easy."

I'm naturally thinking about it a lot but know that things will work out swell. Let nature take its course; and maybe I will hit on a brainstorm that will clear up everything. Thanks a million, Dad, you are really swell to me!

Not much news today, as usual. Just one of those peaceful, lovely, lovely days. Still twenty-two. (missions). We're all feeling fine, especially me lately. Things are just a bit slow around here lately. We are all looking forward to the rest home a lot, and as far as I am concerned, I'd just as leave come home with 22 (missions completed) as anything else.

Enclosed is a request for a few things I could use. —Mom, the candy supply is very good, but I am chewing gum very, very fast, and being that we don't fly as much as usual, my supply is dwindling. That coming Teaberry sounds wonderful (on missions we get a pack of Double-Mint and several candy bars).

Oh, oh, the lights are about to go out so I will have to close for now.

Lots of love to all, Bob

FINALLY, OFF TO THE FLAK HOTEL!

On September 19, Bob and his crew finally got their well-deserved break and headed out for the seaside resort town of Southport on England's northwest coast and over 200 miles from Ridgewell. Their destination was the Birkdale Palace Hotel, now known as the Southport Rest Home.

Like most of England, the town of Southport had been a target of the Luftwaffe's indiscriminate bombing campaign earlier in the war, suffering from nine bombing attacks and 115 air raids. Though there were no major military assets in the town, the German Heinkel and Dornier bombers had dropped incendiary, high-explosive, and parachute bombs with delayed fuses, demolishing and damaging many homes and businesses. In their most infamous strike, the Germans scored a direct hit on Dr. Barnardo's Sunshine Home for Blind Babies. Though by some miracle all twenty-seven blind children survived the bombing, three young nurses perished that night. But slowly, as England gained dominance of their own airspace, the German attacks on less important targets such as Southport subsided. By the time Bob made it to Southport, there hadn't been a bombing attack in three years, and the town had been returned to its prewar beauty.

Accompanying Bob on his trip to Southport were Lieutenants Gene Weisser, Joe Pearce, Mort Yolofsky, Duke Winsor, and Sgt. Bruce Bentley. Bob's enthusiastic letter home, written just one day after his arrival at Southport, offers a firsthand insight into the value and effectiveness of flak hotels.

September 20, 1944

Dear Mom and Dad,

Folks, I hardly know where to start. A lot can be said in a few words though; This is one of the happiest days of my life.

We have been in this gorgeous rest home for a day and already I feel like new. This is nothing short of Shangri-la. Or whatever it's called.

There is just five of us here. Bowman went to visit some friends, leaving Gene, Joe, Mort, Duke, and Bentley (I never see Bent much either because he is very quiet these days).

We are staying at a very nice hotel in a city on the coast near Liverpool. This hotel has been converted into a rest home for combat troops, B-17, and B-24 crews only. Well, it's so nice here. I can't even begin to explain what they are doing for all of us. This place is run by Red Cross girls.

Two men to a large room and Gene (Lieutenant Weisser) and I are together in this fine room, which overlooks the ocean. The beach is beautiful.

The food is like home cooking (or awfully close)—fresh eggs, milk, and everything we ask for.

So, I don't know where to start; after breakfast, Gene, Mort, Duke, and I went to look over the town. Wow! This can't be an English town! Quite large, 20,000, and it compares to St. Petersburg, Florida, to a tee. All the houses are beautiful in appearance and kept up swell.

Oh, if we only had a camera!

The city overlooks the ocean, and all along the beach (behind the beach) is this magnificent park. Their annual flower show ended last week, and the flowers are still in full bloom in this park. Gosh! I can't even begin to describe the beautiful surroundings everywhere.

First thing that caught our eye this morning was a large amusement park, a very close duplicate to our Forest Park Highlands.

Oh, yes! We dress as we care to. There are no MPs here! It feels like we are the only Americans here, and boy do they ever treat us nice! And girls! Oh, my! I had a wonderful date last night—Phew, was she beautiful! No fooling!

I'm going to have a different one every night though, because more than one date with these beauties might result in Robert's being bit by the love bug, and that's bad. And the girls are really nice, coming from all the wealthy families here. (And I do believe everyone in Southport is rich. It's really a resort town.)

We also went rowing in row boats in a lake near our hotel. Then we played nine holes of golf on one of the five beautiful courses here. Next, we took a sightseeing tour in a carriage, horse drawn, like you see in the newsreels of olden times.

. . . I stopped the letter. I had to leave as Gene (Lieutenant Weisser) came in and we went to supper and was it good! After supper Gene and I played records, all the latest hits in the lounge. At 8:00 o'clock also comes a dance in the ballroom arranged by the club here. They have dances three times a week. We met Duke and Joe at the dance, and before long we all had girls and got together and had a wonderful time dancing and talking over our snacks. I walked my girl home after the dance, a country mile, whoa! and when I returned to the hotel, I found Mort (Lt. Yolofsky) writing his nightly letter to his wife.

Tomorrow Gene, Duke (Lieutenant Winsor), and I plan on going horseback riding. The hotel also has stables where we can ride anytime of the day. Also, we are going to play tennis on these beautiful grass courts. Are they ever nice! There are six of them, just like a golf green kept in perfect condition. Also, tomorrow we plan on going swimming in an indoor pool down the road. This must sound fantastic, and even as all these wonderful hours pass, I can hardly believe all the pleasures we've been given. What have we done to deserve all of this? Don't answer that. I think we can all enjoy all of this without a guilty conscience.

> Well folks, I guess it's past my bedtime and I want to get up for those bacon and eggs so I will close for now. Surely thinking of you all a lot more than ever as things here remind me of home so much. Hello and lots of love to Joe and grandma and grandpa. I'll write as often as I can, I could write books every day. I think.
>
> Love to all, Bob

When their weeklong furlough was over, the crew returned directly to base, and the next day they were back in combat, flying a long mission on September 28 to Magdeburg, Germany, just south of Berlin. Joe Pearce was in the pilot's seat; Duke Winsor flew as copilot; Gene Weisser, navigator; Mort Yolofsky, bombardier; Bruce Bentley, radio operator; Charlie Bowman, tail turret gunner; and Bob was back in the belly turret. Seven of the original Florida MacDill crew were now well rested and back together again. That mission to Magdeburg, Bob's twenty-second, went smoothly and was one of those "milk runs" the crew prayed for. Harper:

> We were feeling great after that week in Southport. Things were looking rosy again, I had more than half of my missions behind me, and that first mission when we got back to Ridgewell went swell. I was thinking again that maybe I'd be home for Christmas or, at the very least, be stationed somewhere other than Ridgewell. Little did I suspect that it would take another three more months of combat before I reached my thirty-fifth mission. And months after that to finally catch a ride home to the States.

Nor did Bob suspect that he would be sent on yet another mission to the Leuna Oil Works, where his luck would finally run out and German flak and fighters would knock him out of the sky.

CHAPTER 10
OCTOBER AND THE ENEMY REEMERGES

Mission 23	October 6	Stralsund	43-37791	unnamed B-17
Mission 24	October 7	Zwickau	43-37561	"Rotherhithe's Revenge"
Mission 25	October 14	Cologne	43-37791	unnamed B-17
Mission 26	October 30	Gelsenkirchen	44-6115	"Ice Col' Katy"

With the relaxing week at the rest home behind him, Bob told me that he found himself hoping to quickly notch some more missions. "At that point, it became the more missions, the merrier, and the more milk runs that we could get in, even better. If I could get another month in like July, I might be home for Christmas . . ." But the fall weather turned foul, and eight of the 381st BG's October missions were scrubbed, so like many other airmen that month, Bob's race to get to thirty-five missions turned to a crawl.

In addition to the bad weather making flying more dangerous for the 8th Air Force, they continued to see German fighters. During the first half of 1944, in anticipation of D-day, the Allied forces made it a priority to destroy the German Luftwaffe so that the invasion of France would take place under "friendly skies." To accomplish this, the combined English and American bomber forces hammered every aspect of the Luftwaffe, including airfields and aviation fuel depots, crew and maintenance barracks, airplane factories, and, even more importantly, existing German fighter planes both on the ground and in the skies. Accompanied by hundreds of P-47 and P-51 long-range fighters, many of the heaviest bomber raids of the war were sent against politically important cities such as the German capital, Berlin, as well, knowing that Hitler would be forced to defend them with his dwindling fighter planes. As D-day approached, the 8th Army AF stopped trying to disguise where their bombers were headed. Instead, accompanied by up to a thousand fighters, waves of bombers were used as bait and sent directly at the big German cities and vital industries:

> There also were a number of occasions when tactical surprise was obtained and exploited by our bomber forces with great success. But generally, bomber missions were provocative and purposed with the destruction of any enemy fighters as one of the major objectives.

> It was decided (therefore) that if surprise caused a reduction in the number of enemy fighters intercepting, then efforts to surprise the enemy should be dispensed with since they would reduce potential success. (*8th Air Force Tactical Development, August 1942–May 1945*, Army Air Forces Evaluation Board [ETO])

This nonstop Allied onslaught also began to reduce Germany's valuable core of experienced fighter pilots. By the time of the invasion in June, the Germans were forced to abandon their own bomber force, and their bomber pilots were transitioned to fighter planes. With aviation fuel in scarce supply, new German pilots were getting less than one hundred hours of flight time before being thrown into the fray, while American fighter pilots were averaging over 250 hours before entering combat. Many of these new German fighter pilots were shot down after just a mission or two.

The Allied strategy to decimate the Luftwaffe worked. As the Allied troops hit the beaches in Normandy, the skies above the invasion were devoid of Luftwaffe fighters, and Allied air forces were free to engage in ground support against fixed fortifications as well as interdicting the German reinforcements that were being rushed toward Normandy. But Germany's manufacturing might, determination, and ingenuity seemed undaunted when it came to manufacturing aircraft . . . and for a large part, it went unobserved:

> For months the Allies had been looking on the GAF [German air force] as a beaten arm, capable only of rare and ineffective retaliation. However, Speer's ministry had worked its usual magic. Skillfully mobilizing material and manpower, it concentrated on the Bf 109 and Fw 190 fighter types, and effectively dispersed aircraft production from 27 main plants to 729 smaller ones, some of which were located in quarries, caves, mines, forests, or just in villages. In doing this, the Germans abandoned mass production methods and greatly increased their costs, but they also concealed most of their production centers from both the bombardiers and intelligence officers of the enemy.
>
> In September (1944), the Germans produced 4,103 fighters, their highest total for any month of the war. The Luftwaffe appeared to be poised for a resurgence, although the shortage of fuel and pilots did not allow the operation of nearly as many airplanes as Speer's factories were turning out. (*The Army Air Forces in World War II*, vol. 3, *Europe*)

As a consequence, it wasn't long before the autumn skies above Germany grew dangerous again, and not just because of the increases in dedicated flak defenses; plenty of German fighters were up in the air as well. But as the number of Allied missions and quantities of bombers attacking Germany grew, enemy fighter encounters per any given bomber group were also diluted. Running into these determined German fighter planes became a matter of "the luck of the draw." A good example of this was the fates of two different bomber groups bombing the same target area just days apart. It turns out that Bob's bomber group, the 381st BG, was the luckier of the two.

While Bob and his crewmates were visiting the flak hotel in Southport in September, the 381st BG took part in a raid on Kassel on September 22. According to their squadron combat diary, "Bombing was by PFF, and results were unobserved. Combat men reported meagre to moderate flak and total absence of fighter opposition." However, just five days later the B-24s of the 445th Bomb Group would head for Kassel and get an entirely different result, suffering one of the worst air defeats of the 8th Air Force in the entire war. Here is an abbreviated but firsthand account of the 445th BG's experience, written up in their mission report and copied to the Kassel Memorial Association's website:

> September 27, 1944, Mission to Kassel. It started out uneventfully enough, with 39 planes scheduled to takeoff from our group, the 445th out of Tibenham, England. By the time we got into Germany there had been four aborts, so eventually 35 planes dropped their bombs. The weather over the continent was not very good, with a thick undercast, cloud base about 3,000 feet, and tops 6,000–7,000 feet. It was planned to drop the bombs through the clouds, using the PFF in the lead ship.
>
> The 445th was leading the 2nd Combat Wing, the other groups in the wing being the 389th BG and the 453rd BG. . . . But Major McCoy decided to continue east and bomb the city of Gottingen, about 50 miles away (the radar man and navigator of the 445th had missed a turn). As a result, we lost our fighter escort, and flew alone to our own destruction. Some of the pilots contacted the lead ship to report the error, but the only signal they received was "Keep it tight—Keep it together."
>
> We carried on east, and finally dropped our bombs at Gottingen. We then made a turn to the south, and in the vicinity of Eisenach, we made a right turn to proceed west. By this time, we were probably

> a hundred miles behind the rest of the division. Just as we made the turn, we were attacked from the rear by between 100 and 150 German fighters. They attacked us line abreast in three waves. Most of these fighters were specially adapted Fw 190s equipped with extra armor, and both 20 and 30 mm cannons. They were accompanied by a smaller number of Me 109s.
>
> The battle probably lasted only a few minutes, but it was a horrendous attack, as the Fw 190 assault fighters passed through the bomber formations with 20 and 30 mm cannons blazing, and the .50 machine guns of the B-24s responding. The skies were full of bright flashes from the exploding shells.
>
> When the smoke of this great battle had cleared, 25 of our bombers had crashed into German soil. Two of our planes crash-landed in occupied France. One had crashed near Brussels, Belgium. Two made it across the Channel to make forced landings at the emergency strip at Mansion. One crashed near the base in Norfolk. Only four were able to land at Tibenham.
>
> Of the 238 men aboard the 25 bombers which went down in Germany, 115 were KIA or subsequently died of injuries. One was killed in the plane which crashed in Norfolk, and one was killed in the crash in Belgium, for a total of 117. Perhaps because they had lost the battle, the 8th Air Force did not circulate news of this failed raid with its devastating losses. (Kassel Memorial site)

On Bob's next mission, October 7, 1944, his crew flew the "Rotherhithe's Revenge" to Zwickau. Although they returned to base unscathed, the 381st BG combat diary told the story of a damaged B-17 that had accompanied them. The B-17 took over two hundred flak hits but still managed to return to Ridgewell:

> They were flying in a Fortress called "Pella Tulip." Two minutes before bombs away, the "Tulip" was hit by a flak burst which virtually shattered the nose and cockpit and knocked the bomber out of formation. 1Lt. Charles W. Reseigh, the pilot, hit in both arms and in the face by flak bursts and suffering from a broken leg also caused by a flak wound, was too seriously hurt to pull the bomber out of its dive. 1Lt. David R. Rautio, the copilot, had also been knocked out by the blast. He regained consciousness, pulled the ship out of its dive when it was low enough to avoid anoxia difficulties (the oxygen system had been knocked out), and salvoed the bomb load.

For the next four hours Rautio fought with the stubborn Fortress, despite the streaming cold of the open cockpit and despite his wound, nursed it back to England with both its right-side engines out. Rautio sustained injuries of the forehead and of the right arm. TSgt. John M. Nushy, the engineer and top turret gunner, put out a fire in the cockpit, helped remove the pilot to the radio room, where the bombardier administered first aid, and then Nushy climbed into the pilot's seat, where he acted as copilot for Rautio, intermittently massaging Rautio's face and neck to minimize danger to the 21-year-old Rautio from frostbite. Nushy suffered mainly from conjunctivitis, caused by the flying plexiglass when the nose was shattered. Winicki, the navigator, was credited with excellent work throughout the grueling trip. He and Nushy narrowly escaped serious injury when Winicki stooped down for a flak helmet, at Rautio's order, and Nushy bent down at the same moment to check a flaw in his oxygen equipment. A flak burst slammed right past the spot their heads had been.

On October 30, Bob flew on the "Ice Col' Katy" and witnessed another one of the bombers in his squadron in big trouble. The 533rd Combat Squadron war diary detailed the loss of these crewmen despite the B-17 returning safely to base:

> The final mission of the month, Oct. 30, had Gelsenkirchen as its target and our 37 aircraft were under command of Capt. MacNeill. The weather was 10/10, again, keeping the record intact for the month. Moreover, dense, persistent contrails bothered the fliers. The formation bombed the marshalling yards at Hamm, the secondary target using PFF (Radio Pathfinder Force) methods. There was meager and inaccurate flak seen at the target, but none of it was near us. We saw no enemy fighters. There was no battle damage, for a change. Yet, strangely enough, we lost two men. The two, both members of Lt. Berkley's crew, bailed out over the English Channel on the way to the target when the No. 1 engine caught fire and the bomber went out of control. Lt. Berkley eventually righted his ship and brought it back. Missing are: 1Lt. Harry L. Delaplane Jr., bombardier, and SSgt. Frank K. Gunderson, tail gunner.

During combat, whenever a B-17 filled with smoke or spun out of control, the crew often made individual split-second decisions whether to bail out and try to parachute to safety. Though there were bailout alarms, the gunners (especially) knew that if their pilots had been wounded or killed in the attack, they might have to sort this out for themselves. This was especially true for the tail turret and belly turret gunners, who had separate escape hatches that they could take advantage of. After a few missions, most B-17 crewmen would have witnessed planes go down with the entire crew still on board, so some reacted quicker than they needed to, and it wasn't rare to hear of a plane returning to base battle-damaged and missing a man or two who had parachuted for safety.

In the case of Lt. Berkley's crew, two of his men made that decision and jumped out of their B-17 while it was "temporarily out of control." The rescue teams never found Delaplane or Gunderson, and it was assumed that both men had perished in the ice-cold waters. For the many men who witnessed those two parachutists jumping from that plane, a plane that would eventually make its way safely back to base? Well, they could add this twist of fate to the many ways that you could die in the dangerous skies above Europe.

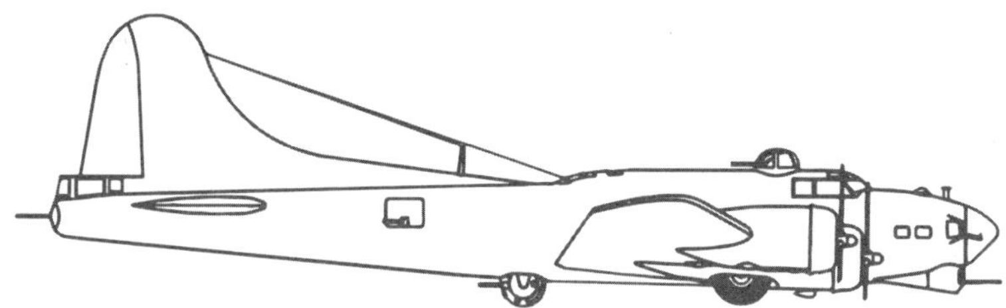

The newly minted triple-wing Barling Bomber, the world's largest airplane, heads for the 1923 St. Louis Air Show. Two years later the Barling Bomber would be scrapped for failing to gain enough altitude (6,500 feet) to traverse the Appalachian Mountains. *US Army Air Service, public domain*

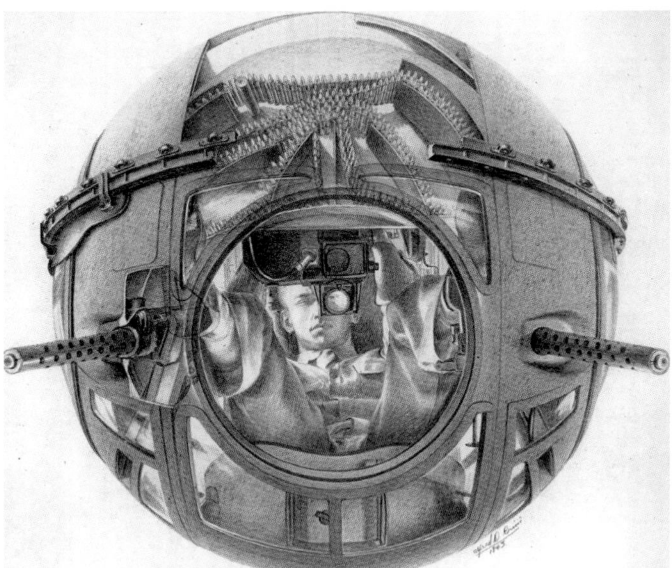

This illustration showing the B-17 ball turret appeared in ***Life*** magazine, January 24, 1944. Jutting out on either side of a round Plexiglas window, the twin .50-caliber M2 gun barrels were air-cooled by the subfreezing ambient temperatures and slipstream of the bomber's 180 mph cruising speed. Note that this gunner is wearing his dress khakis and a tie instead of his normal bulky flight suit! *Alfred D. Crimi, illustration for US Army advertisement, public domain*

On his way to MacDill Air Force Base for combat crew training, Pvt. Bob Harper stopped in St. Louis to say a final goodbye to his family. Bob poses with "Petti," the family cocker spaniel. *Harper family collection*

Ordnance crew preparing to load bombs, July 1944. On a typical 381st BG mission, three of its squadrons flying a dozen B-17s would each require the safe loading of hundreds of bombs, with the work often done in the rain and half dark. *Courtesy of Fold3*

Back Row Left to Right	Front Row Left To Right
Sgt. Charles Bowman (Top Turret Gunner) Greencastle, Pa.	Sgt. Clifford R. Shirley (Waist Gunner) East Point, Ga.
Lt. Morton Yolofsky (Bombardier) Newark, N.J.	Cpl. Henry Fleming (Tail Gunner) Yountville, Calif.
Lt. Joseph J. Pearce, Jr (Pilot) Milford, Del.	Sgt, Bruce Bently (Radio Operator) Peoria, Ill.
Lt. Dale Winsor (Co-Pilot) Morris, Ill.	Cpl. Robert Harper (Ball Turret Gunner) St. Louis, Mo.
Lt. Eugene Weisser (Navigator) Pittsburgh, Pa.	Cpl. Glen Studebaker (Waist Gunner) Silver Springs, Md.

Bob Harper and his crewmates pose at MacDill Army Base in Florida, fall 1944, before leaving for their final training phase in Georgia and subsequent posting in England. The geographic assortment of their hometowns was typical for an American bomber crew. *Harper family collection*

Mistakes could be as deadly as flak and German fighters. On Bob's second mission to Cologne, nearby B-17 "hell's angel" was badly damaged when a Fortress flying above her dislodged three stuck bombs, two of them striking the nose of "hell's angel" and killing their navigator 1Lt. Drummond. *Courtesy of Fold3*

Bob's crew would fly their fourteenth mission to heavily defended Munich on "Dream Baby," *shown above*, the first of the 381st's B-17s to successfully reach one hundred combat missions. *US Army photograph, courtesy of Freeman collection*

Stephen Crane's novel about the Civil War and a young private who flees the battle has never been out of print. Deserting your B-17 bomber could also have major consequences for any crewman whose nerve failed him. This cover of *Red Badge of Courage* is just one of dozens that have been used over the years.

By the fall of 1944, flak was taking down more B-17s than enemy fighters. The ball turret gunner of the "Little Miss Mischief," Sgt. Ed Abno, survived this burst of flak but was unable to climb out of the belly turret until the plane made a successful landing back at base. He subsequently lost a toe to frostbite. *Courtesy of Fold3*

The 5-foot, 4-inch belly turret gunner Bob Harper and the 6-foot, 6-inch waist gunner Gene Studebaker mug for camera outside their Nissen hut. *Harper family collection*

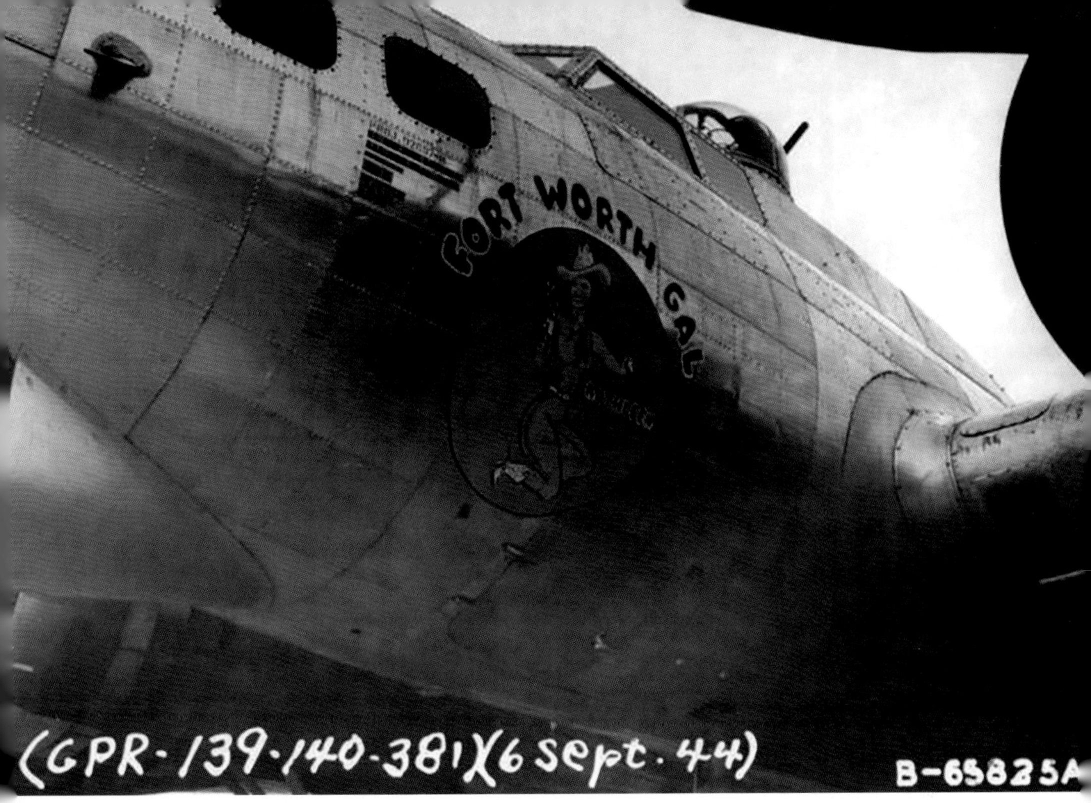
FORT WORTH GAL
(GPR-139-140-381)(6 Sept. 44)
B-65825A

On August 27, Bob's crew flew the "Fort Worth Gal" on a mission to Berlin. Just two weeks later, with a different crew on board, the "Fort Worth Gal" ran into enemy fighters over Neiburg, Germany, and was shot down. *Courtesy of Fold3*

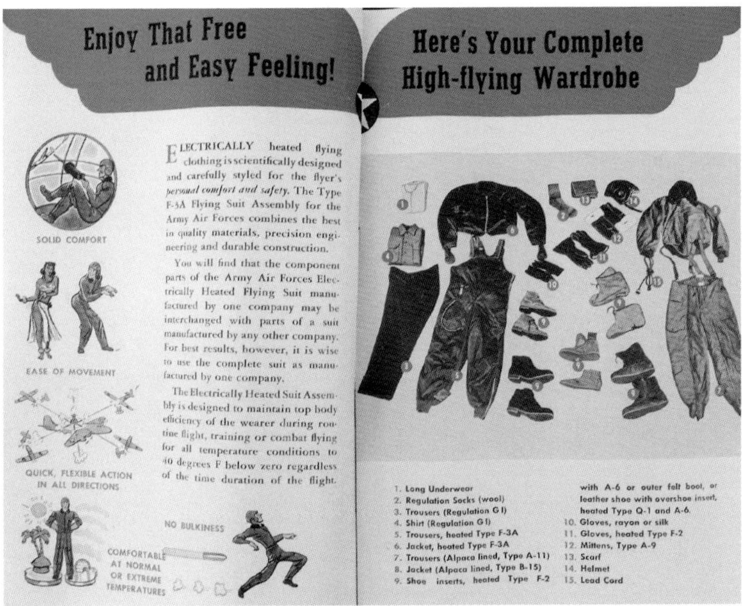

Enjoy That Free and Easy Feeling!
ELECTRICALLY heated flying clothing is scientifically designed and carefully styled for the flyer's *personal comfort and safety.* The Type F-3A Flying Suit Assembly for the Army Air Forces combines the best in quality materials, precision engineering and durable construction.
You will find that the component parts of the Army Air Forces Electrically Heated Flying Suit manufactured by one company may be interchanged with parts of a suit manufactured by any other company. For best results, however, it is wise to use the complete suit as manufactured by one company.
The Electrically Heated Suit Assembly is designed to maintain top body efficiency of the wearer during routine flight, training or combat flying for all temperature conditions to 40 degrees F below zero regardless of the time duration of the flight.
SOLID COMFORT
EASE OF MOVEMENT
QUICK, FLEXIBLE ACTION IN ALL DIRECTIONS
NO BULKINESS
COMFORTABLE AT NORMAL OR EXTREME TEMPERATURES
Here's Your Complete High-flying Wardrobe
1. Long Underwear
2. Regulation Socks (wool)
3. Trousers (Regulation G I)
4. Shirt (Regulation G I)
5. Trousers, heated Type F-3A
6. Jacket, heated Type F-3A
7. Trousers (Alpaca lined, Type A-11)
8. Jacket (Alpaca lined, Type B-15)
9. Shoe inserts, heated Type F-2 with A-6 or outer felt boot, or leather shoe with overshoe insert, heated Type Q-1 and A-6.
10. Gloves, rayon or silk
11. Gloves, heated Type F-2
12. Mittens, Type A-9
13. Scarf
14. Helmet
15. Lead Cord

Frostbite was a constant enemy of B-17 gunners operating in environments that could reach –50°F and colder. Bob's Model F-3 General Electric flying suit came with a six-page manual. The F-3 was the third-iteration heated suit and included a double circuit in the heat liner layer in case one shorted out or was damaged. *General Electric Instruction Manual 1943*

B-17 "Honey," 42-0007, was Bob's favorite B-17. This photo, dated April 11, 1944, was taken while the "Honey" was still undergoing major repairs to correct the extensive damage incurred on a combat mission two weeks prior. *Courtesy of Fold3*

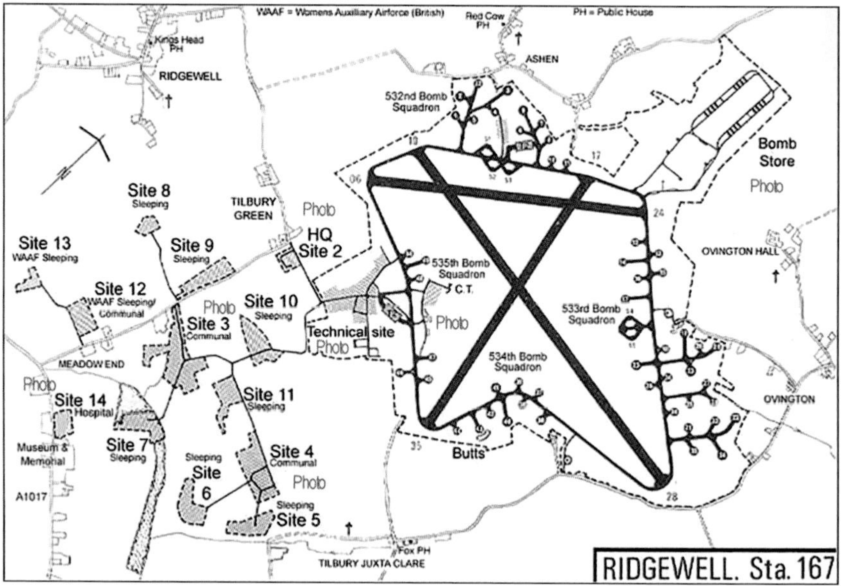

Diagram of Ridgewell Airfield. Located in the countryside of East Anglia, Ridgewell's facilities and three runways were spread out over 600 acres. *Public domain*

Shown in a faded snapshot from eighty years ago, the scavenged carcass of B-17 "Honey" sitting in a field in Belgium and being used as a photo prop by five townspeople and their dog. The lettering "Honey" is still eligible on her nose. *Courtesy of Rudy Kenis*

Returning from a bombing run to the heavily defended Leuna Synthetic Oil Works in Merseburg on September 11, 1944, Bob's crew poses in front of the "Rotherhithe's Revenge." Bob is kneeling, *front row, second from left. Harper family collection*

Taken over by the American Red Cross in 1942, the Birkdale Palace Hotel in Southport, England, served as a rehabilitation center or "Flak Hotel" for over 15,000 USAAF personnel during World War II.

Crewmates Bentley and Bowman pose with their gun barrels after a mission to Gelsenkirchen on October 30, 1944. In the background is the "Ice Col' Katy," one of the fourteen B-17s that Bob flew into combat. "Ice Col' Katy" was named after a popular 1943 dance tune by singer Hattie McDaniel. *Harper family collection*

On July 31, 1944, the US Army ran a full-page recruitment ad in *Life* magazine, featuring the 381st's B-17 "Winsome Winn" despite the fact that she had already been shot down. Paintings rather than photos were often used to soften war scenes in recruitment ads but were also a mainstay of wartime advertising by the likes of Studebaker, General Motors, and Boeing Aircraft, which used them to tout their contribution to manufacturing America's heavy bombers. *US Army recruitment ad, 1944, public domain*

The B-17 "Winsome Winn" headed for combat passes over a patchwork of farms near the Ridgewell Base. *Courtesy of Fold3*

November 19, 1944. Col. Leber, 381st BG commander, presents Sgt. Bob Harper with the Distinguished Flying Cross. Two days later, Bob would be shot down on his fourth mission to Merseburg. *Harper family collection*

B-17 "Colonel Bub." There is no record of who "Colonel Bub" was, but the use of "Bub," meaning friend or buddy, was widespread in the 1940s. Best guess? In a famous 1943 Bugs Bunny cartoon about US bombers, Bugs coined the phrase "What's all the hubbub, bub?" *Courtesy of Fold3*

The B-17 "Colonel Bub" landed itself on autopilot in an empty farm field after Bob's crew parachuted to safety. *Harper family collection*

Top row: gunner Bob Harper and navigator Gene Weisser; *bottom row*, bombardier Mort Yolofsky and pilot Joe Pearce. These four friends would fly together for one last time on October 14, 1944. Each man would log over three hundred hours of combat time during their time with the 533rd Bomb Squadron. *Harper family collection*

Bob would fly his last combat mission, number 35, to Remagen, Germany, on the "Fort Lansing Emancipator." *Courtesy of Fold3*

Shooting craps on base at Ridgewell. "We staged a few of these photos just for laughs! Not sure if any of the guys in my crew really gambled much, except each morning when we climbed aboard that B-17!" remembered Bob Harper. *Harper family collection*

CHANUTE FIELD IDENTIFICATION CARD AND PASS

Name Harper, Robert H Date 5-31-45

Grade S/Sgt. Sec. C, 3502d B.U.

RIGHT THUMB PRINT

R-1008

SIGNATURE

A.S.N. 37618149

Age 22

Weight 125

Eyes Blue

Hair Blond

HARPER 37618149

R 1008

Authentication

RANK TITLE [illegible]P. BURKHARTSMEIER, 1st Lt [illegible]

Chanute Field ID pass. Throughout the war, the Army kept Bob at exactly 125 pounds, despite weighing 110 pounds at his first physical and arriving home "frightfully thin" according to his mother. The minimum weight for a soldier at the time was 125 pounds. *Harper family collection*

Bob and Katy on their first date, St. Louis, Missouri, 1946. *Harper family collection*

Bob Harper, taking photos for a marketing campaign at the Nooter Company. *Harper family collection*

Featured on this US commemorative stamp was the 381st BG's "Flak Happy," painted by aviation artist Bill Phillips of Ashland, Oregon. *Bill Cullen photo*

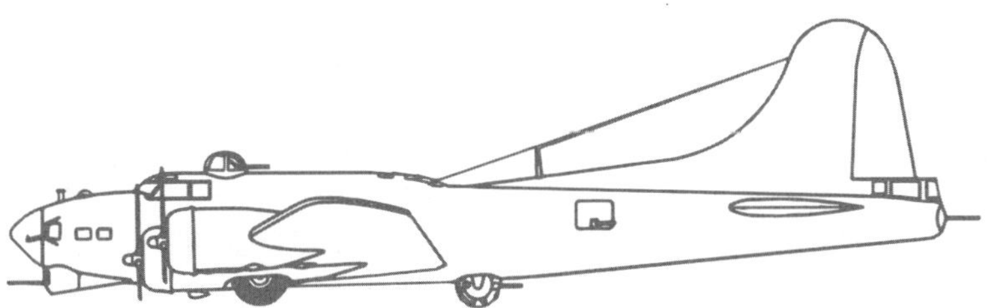

CHAPTER 11
COMBAT, REAL AND IMAGINED

> Our attempt to make good on the extravagant ads appearing in the home press was pretty much a flop! Full-page art jobs in *Time* and *Life* proclaimed that the Fortress, in addition to its other virtues, was now equipped to carry ten tons of bombs. What an airplane: it could fly at 40,000 feet, carry ten tons, do 300 miles an hour, fly 3,000 miles. Poor Public. They were never told that it could do any one of those three things, but it couldn't do any two of them at the same time. Sure, it was a fine airplane—the finest in the world, as we darn well know, but we also know its limitations.
>
> —1st Combat Wing mission report

After spending several years researching Bob's time at Ridgewell, I became quick to notice photos of B-17s when they were featured in old magazines and journals from the World War II era . . . and even quicker when I spotted that telltale "L in a triangle" on the tail, indicating the aircraft was from Bob's 381st Bomb Group. One afternoon as I perused an old issue of *Life* magazine (July 1944), I noticed a full-page recruitment ad for the 8th Army Air Force that claimed, "You'll Go Places on This Team." Centered in the ad was a painting of four young airmen, calmly recounting a mission in the B-17 "Winsome Winn." A second, smaller painting was placed in the corner of the ad, a watercolor of a B-17 under attack by five "Jerry" fighters. I enlarged the drawing of the B-17 on my computer screen and found the telltale L in a triangle. Bingo! The 381st BG!

The *Life* advertisement was directed at boys, *Men of 17!* who might be thinking about a future enlistment in the Army. The copywriter did his job of making air combat sound exciting as he described the mission!:

> First Lieutenant Richard J Niederriter, pilot, 1st Lieutenant Richard A. Carocari, navigator Sergeant Richard W Evans, tail gunner and first Lieutenant Lester A Darst Bombardier have hit most of Germany's hotspots in their flying fortress the Winsome Winn. Asked which was their most exciting mission their answer was unanimous, Anklam. "You probably never heard of Anklam,"

Lieutenant Carocari said. "Before the war it was just a little jerk-water town 100 miles from Berlin. But the Nazis built a Focke-Wulf assembly plant there. And our assignment was to flatten it."

"I plotted my course for Berlin, to make Jerry think that was where we were heading. And we hadn't any more than crossed Denmark until the reception committee buzzed out to meet us. At least 300 German fighters hit our flight. They came barreling in from all directions at once. The fire from their cannons and machine guns making a solid sheet of flame along their wings. The going was hot and heavy for a while."

"Hot and heavy is right," Lieutenant Niederriter said. "We were under fire for 3½ hours. But our Gunners were too smart and too good for them. Evans here had his tail gun knocked out so he came up and fired the flexible gun in the nose. When the ball turret got fouled up with oil from a damaged line the ball gunner adjusted it so it would keep revolving to fool the fighters and then he climbed out and lent a hand at the waist guns. It was the prettiest piece of teamwork I've ever seen."

"That's what really licked them," Sergeant Evans said, "team-work! Lieutenant Niederriter had his hands full keeping up the Winsome Winn on her course . . . but the whole time he sat up there and called the shots for us Gunners. We sure did work those German fighters over. We saw two of them blow up in mid-air."

"Finally," Lieutenant Darst said, "we changed our course and cut for Anklam. The Focke-Wulfs gave us a breathing spell as we swung up over the town and we made a nice smooth bombing run. I saw our eggs land square on that factory. And brother did we plaster it! They won't make fighter planes there very soon again."

Lieutenant Niederriter grinned. "Sure," he said. "You go plenty of places in the AAF. And it's not exactly joy riding either. But we've got a job to do and we work together to do it.

"You're on a team in the AAF. From the time you step into your first training plane until you get up there in the action. And it's a winning team . . . an unbeatable team . . . the 'greatest team in the world.'" (AAF recruitment ad, 1944)

I had read some harrowing tales of air combat, and this narrative didn't seem close to reality. I couldn't imagine any of Bob's crew ever recounting a story like that with such bravado. Little things stuck out; could a ball turret be set on automatic without a gunner inside, especially with the hydraulic oil leaking? Would the German fighters be fooled (or even care) if they saw a belly turret spinning around? And since when did a gunner stand around after a mission, with 40-pound belts of live ammunition looped around his neck like a bandola in a Hollywood western? From what I had read, most of the men stripped off their sweat-soaked, uncomfortable flying suits as soon as possible and headed for a shot of whisky at the debriefing . . . but this copywriter had turned their frightening, life-and-death struggle into something that seemed more like the shoot-out at the OK Corral. After the harrowing combat mission described in the *Life* ad, the crew would be praying to never see a "Jerry" fighter again.

I dug deeper and quickly discovered that B-17 23078, "Winsome Winn," was in fact a real bomber assigned to the 381st BG, 334th Bomb Squadron. On October 9, it was one of the sixteen B-17s from the 381st that participated on that Anklam raid. According to the 534th Squadron combat diary, it was a tough mission:

> Six of our Fortresses took off at 0803 to participate in the longest raid yet. This time it was Anklam, Germany. Today's target was the important Arado Aircraft Components factory located just off the center of the town. Crews stated that they had a good bomb run and observed the mean point of impact to be saturated with bursts. AA Fire was moderate on way in, becoming intense over the target. Again, the Germans threw up everything they had in fighters. Our crews stuck by their guns and accounted for 5 enemy aircraft destroyed, 2 probably destroyed, and 3 as damaged. . . . For the second day in a row, we [the 534th Squadron] suffered the loss of a plane and crew. Lt. J. L. Loftin and crew are reported missing in action. Cause, time, and place of loss are still unknown.

The 242nd Medical Detachment's diary shed even more light:

> At 1200 hours, 16 B-17s from this command took off with the target the Focke-Wulf factory at Anklam, Germany. The Target is thought to have been destroyed. The greater part of the flight was over the North Sea, and three aircraft failed to return to base.

Then, after listing each name and rank of the twenty-two men killed in action that day and listing the eight men who were probable POWs, the doctor, Col. Gaillard, continued:

Lt. Loftins' crew was seen to parachute over Germany. Lt. Carqueville left the formation somewhere in enemy territory. Maj. Hendricks was on his return trip over the North Sea and apparently felt he was out of the fighter zone and left the formation. He was jumped by fighters and was seen to lose altitude rapidly, and estimates of four to six parachutes were seen to leave the ship. Some crews reported the aircraft ditched, and one reported that the ship exploded just before it hit the water. However, it should be pointed out that the aircraft were flying at approximately 15,000 feet, and assuming that Maj. Hendricks' aircraft was in control, the distance between the formation and the ship as it reached sea level would be at least 20–30 miles, consequently the accuracy of the observation may be questioned.

Four other men were also missing, from the 532nd BS. . . . Apparently, just as the formation was reaching the Danish coast, a 20 mm cannon shell exploded in the cockpit of Lt. Douglas Winters' ship, and he was temporarily stunned or blinded by the flash. When he came to, the bombardier and navigator had already left the ship, the co-pilot was jumping, and one of the crew members gave him a farewell salute and jumped.

The ship was in a steep gliding turn and there was a fire in the rear of the cockpit. Lt. Winters righted the ship, put on the automatic pilot, went back, and put out the fire, and then brought the ship safely back to England, landing at another base. He suffered a mild flash burn of the face. He was the only one in the forward part of the ship, and the courage and determination and skill that he displayed has been the basis for recommendation of a high military award.

In the last two days this group has lost ten aircraft and many old, experienced crews, and the effect has been demoralizing to the staff and the combat crews. We all feel these losses very keenly, and smiles and apparently cheerfulness are forced, and everyone is quite well aware of the others' feelings. The loss of two squadron commanders, majors Ingenhutt and Hendricks, has especially affected us, both from the standpoint of morale and administration.

Had the copywriter used those details, it is doubtful if anyone would have rushed to volunteer to train on a B-17. Though no one can blame the Army for jazzing up the Anklam raid in their recruitment advertisement, flying in a B-17 on a combat mission during the fall of 1943 was one of the most dangerous places in the world to be for an American soldier:

In October 1943, fewer than one out of four 8th Air Force crew members could expect to complete his tour of duty: twenty-five combat missions. The statistics were discomforting: two-thirds of the men could expect to die in combat or be captured by the enemy. And 17% would either be wounded seriously, suffer a disabling mental breakdown, or die in a violent air accident over English soil. . . . By the end of the war, the 8th Air Force would have more fatal casualties, 26,000, then the entire United States Marine Corps. Seventy-seven percent of the Americans who flew against the Reich before D-Day would wind up casualties." (Donald Miller, *Masters of the Air*)

What was also interesting (and in this case, sadly ironic) was how little "real time" information was shared during the war. On January 7, 1944, three months after the Anklam raid, the "Winsome Winn" was shot down. A full six months after her demise, the "Winsome Winn" was used in that *Life* recruitment advertisement! The copywriter obviously had no idea of the plane's true fate.

As I looked further into the history of the "Winsome Winn," I was surprised to discover the story of her last mission, detailed in an article in the *New York Times*:

EX-GUNNER SPOTS A MODEL OF HIS B-17, DOWNED IN '44

August 15, 1982, by David W Dunlap

Robert J. Geraghty stepped onto Rockefeller Plaza yesterday morning and was transported back 38 years to the skies over Germany. Mr. Geraghty, an investigator on Rockefeller Center's security staff, had gone out to take a look at the hundred or so model aircraft on display outside the RCA Building.

What caught his attention was the replica of a B-17 bomber with a 6-foot 10-inch wingspan—his aircraft in World War II. More than that, he said, the model's tail marking was a black L in a white triangle, the insignia of the 381st Bomb Group—his group. "I'm Numb With This."

And far more than that, the name painted on the nose of the four-engine airplane was "Winsome Winn," lost in a bombing run over the I.G. Farben factories in Ludwigshafen in 1944—his ship.

> Mr. Geraghty, a 60-year-old Brooklyn resident who is a retired New York City mounted police officer, pointed to the tiny figures in the "Winsome Winn" cockpit. "This is Arden D. Wilson, the pilot," he said. The bomber was named after the pilot's wife, Winnie . . .
>
> The original "Winsome Winn" had flown 34 missions over Germany when it left England with a crew of 10 on Jan. 7, 1944. Sergeant Geraghty was the ball-turret gunner, under the bomber's fuselage.
>
> "We were over the target," Mr. Geraghty said. "We got direct flak in the No. 1 engine and dropped out of formation. The fighters hit us in the No. 2 engine. When the plane slipped, the plume of fire between the two engines whipped around and enveloped my ball turret."
>
> "The radioman and the tail gunner were both killed," he said. "I dropped 25,000 feet, locked in the ball turret. I bailed out at 3,000 feet."
>
> "We were captured immediately," he said, and held in Stalag 17 until V-E Day. Mr. Geraghty said he keeps four telegrams—all sent to his mother—that had charted his ordeal. The first reported that he was missing. The second reported that he was a prisoner. The third that he had been returned. The fourth that he was back in the United States.

Real air combat took many shapes and forms. One of the most unusual combat events that happened to a 381st BG aircrew took place in the skies right above their home airfield and was captured by a pilot with the 534th Squadron. In a passage written in his unpublished journal, *Recollections of a Florida Cracker*, Lt. Troy Smith illustrated how dangerous it was to crew a B-17 during World War II. You were never safe until you were on the ground and your engines switched off. Returning from an aborted mission to destroy a vital bridge in France, Lt. Smith came under friendly fire and was forced to land his damaged B-17 while fully loaded with bombs:

> That day we carried extra-high explosive bombs called RDX. Because the bombs had to be right on that target to do any damage, we needed to bomb visually. However, after we had reached the IP and turned on our bomb run, a large cloud moved in and completely obliterated the target. We did a 360-degree turn, again departed the IP and started down the bomb run again, when unfortunately, the same thing happened again. By that time the flack was getting pretty darn heavy and as the sky was more than 50% covered with

clouds, the Wing Leader decided to head for home. I was flying group lead and tucked into the formation. As we circled Ridgewell with the formation intact, elements of three bombers were peeling off for landings. Six ships were still in formation, my two wing men behind and below us was the lead element.

All of a sudden, POW!!! An explosion in the cockpit. Hydraulic fluid spewed on my goggles and windshield, completely covering the cockpit. My copilot jumped out of his seat, headed down below to the hatch, and yelled, "Let's get out of here!" As I was flying the plane and could feel it responding well to the controls, I grabbed him by the shoulder and said, "Let's wait a minute and see what happens." Actually, the only serious thing that happened was that we lost our hydraulic fluid and now had no brakes.

I called the tower and asked if I could fly out over the North Sea and drop the RDX bombs, as I didn't particularly relish landing with a bomb bay full of high explosives and no brakes. The tower said, "Stand by," and went into a huddle with somebody.

After ten minutes or so they finally came back on air and said, "No, don't salvo your bombs. Just wait until everyone else has landed and you'll get clearance to land." They didn't want to waste the RDXs, which were in short supply, and they didn't want me messing up the runway (if we crashed and blew up) until the other planes had landed. But the other planes did land, and I finally got clearance to follow them on in.

I lined up, came in low, and tried to land as short as possible on the runway. As soon as we touched down, I cut the inboard engines and let the plane slow down. As I didn't want to run off the far end of the runway, I called for the tailwheel to be unlocked, gave a little power to the #4 engine, and turned into the soft soil to the left of the runway. The plane rolled a little farther than I expected, and as it happened, we were headed directly for the control tower (with a full load of bombs aboard). With considerable excitement in his voice, the tower operator yelled over the radio, "That's far enough! That's far enough!"

Under my breath I muttered, "Scream, you SOB; you wouldn't let me drop these bombs in the sea."

When we got in for our debriefing, Berg (Lieutenant Aikenhead), who had been flying bombardier in the element lead bomber, just behind and below us, walked up to the table where my crew was

> being questioned and said, "You know what happened? When I went to clear the nose turret, I accidentally hit the trigger and sprayed you with my .50 calibers."
>
> Those rounds had gone through my horizontal stabilizer, worked their way up through the bomb bay, just missing the RDX bombs by inches, and came on up through the cockpit, hitting and exploding the hydraulic accumulator.

The bombardier's carelessness that day could have ended the lives of those nine crewmen in the B-17 flying above him. His errant .50 rounds had just missed two of the bombs and a fuel tank and struck just inches from where the two pilots sat. Tragedies involving friendly fire can be found in all the combat histories of the forty bomber groups stationed in England.

According to Smith's journal, his crew managed to laugh it off as just another close call. There were no consequences for Lt. Aikenhead that I could find in official rccords.

I eventually got around to asking Bob what combat was like when they were attacked by fighters, and if he had ever shot down a German fighter:

> Well, I shot at more than a few of those German fighters; that was my job. I don't think our crew ever claimed specifically that we got one. Never made that claim. One reason was that everything happened up there at incredible speed during combat. I don't think people get that. If a fighter dove through our formation, it was moving at 360 mph (or 528 feet per second), and then we had our own speed, that could be 180 mph or so, so add that to it, and you get what is called closing speed, and that could easily hit 540 mph or more. Usually, there would be several B-17s firing simultaneously at each fighter, so along with my own two .50s, maybe a half-dozen guns or more trying to hit it from our B-17 alone, and possibly more fire coming from our wingmen.
>
> And we didn't have gun cameras, to answer your question about that. You did your job and got the attacking fighters in your automatic gunsights and held them there as long as you could . . . and squeezed off your guns in short bursts . . . but that could be for as little as a second or at most two or three seconds. And then they were out of effective range of my guns.

Of course, if a fighter was attacking directly from behind, then with my two guns and the tail gunners' two, we would have a much-better shot at him because of the very slow closing speed. (Figure the fighter speed of 360 mph minus a B-17 speed of 160 to 180 mph, so instead of 540 mph that happened from the frontal attacks, only 200 mph or so.) So, if they came from the rear, they would have put themselves in our gunsights for much longer. Probably explains why they rarely came at us from directly behind, at least while I was serving combat, because of course the Germans learned early on what worked and what didn't. . . . The Germans made a science out of attacking the heavy bombers, knew our zones of fire probably as well as we did. . . . We tried to do the same with them, make a science of defending our bombers. We did it through the setup of our formations and the interlocking fields of fire.

On some days we were called to lectures, or what we called drills, where we would spend time in front of a screen of fighters or attack scenarios and talk shop about what the Germans might do, their updated fighters and new tactics as well. And as I've mentioned, the introduction of the long-range fighters to accompany us was the big game changer. *Our little buddies.* That started before I got to Ridgewell. Of course, fighter escort never helped out with the flak; that was all ours to deal with.

Okay, I know you want an answer to your question; I never claimed that I shot down a fighter, but there was one time when a German fighter blew up in my gunsights. There could have been two or three other machine guns firing at it, so who knows; it was over in a flash. So, there was that. I really don't remember what mission or any other details of that day. Funny, but I also don't remember seeing the German fighter that took out one of our engines on our way into Merseburg the day we got shot down, I think we barely got a glimpse of him. . . . You could feel the cannon shell hit the plane, the plane shudder for a few seconds, but we managed to keep up with the squadron until we got to the target, to Merseburg. Then we got hit again.

Yep, I saw the German fighter blow up in my gunsight.

Bob grew silent, lost in memories, no doubt, so I decided to change the subject and talk about what was happening in my life for a change and what was going on with the nearby forest fires that were threatening

Portland, Oregon, at the time. Talking about shooting at other people was just not his favorite subject. Like so many others who fought in the war, Bob was a reluctant hero who took no joy in the necessary killing that was taking place above and below.

Which brings me back to the "Winsome Winn." The Niederriter crew of the "Winsome Winn" did their job that day of the Anklam raid with great success and lived to fight another day. Months later, another crew fought just as bravely in that same bomber, only to be shot down. If I learned one thing from my time researching Bob's book and reading dozens of accounts of World War II air combat, most authors who were in the thick of the fight concluded that it eventually came down to luck.

If you climbed into a B-17 for a combat mission, you were as brave as those men who had preceded you the day before, and as brave as those men who would follow you the next day. Though the skills and training of your team were critical to increasing the odds of survival, they would keep you alive flying in those flak fields only until your luck ran out. And thankfully for many men, their luck never did run out.

CHAPTER 12
MEDAL DAY

Mission 27	November 5	Frankfurt	42-97059	"Marsha Sue"
Mission 28	November 6	Hamburg	42-97357	"the Railroader"
Mission 29	November 9	Oeuvres-Chesney	42-31761	"Rotherhithe's Revenge"
Mission 30	November 10	Cologne	42-98782	unnamed B-17

Bob Harper:

> I turned the page of my old calendar, and it was November 1944! Hard to believe, but I was starting my fifth month of combat. The crew was still okay, but Southport and the flak hotel now seemed like a lifetime ago. . . . October had been a bad month, and with those dangerous winter skies to deal with, it was getting harder to fly tight formations. Some days the flak seemed worse than ever . . . then Joe wound up back in the flak hotel. A sign of the times.

When November rolled around, the skies above Europe had cleared up enough for Bob to find himself in the air again, flying four missions in just six days. On the first of those missions, Bob flew on the B-17 "Marsha Sue" to Frankfurt. On board were five of his old Florida crew, and the bomber was piloted by Lt. Duke Winsor.

Much like the previous month, the Germans were now engaged in a desperate battle as they slowly retreated toward their homeland. The 8th AF's scrubbed missions and stand-downs of October had given the Germans time to strengthen and rebuild their flak defenses, and though the 381st returned from the Frankfurt mission with all thirty-seven of their planes, four of them were badly battle-damaged.

The following day, Bob stepped aboard the B-17 nicknamed "the Railroader" for the fifth time and flew to Hamburg. This time the 381st BG was not as lucky, losing two of their thirty-seven bombers. The mission report from the 381st combat diary told the story:

> We went back to Hamburg November 6 with Capt. Frank L. Tyson, 535th Squadron operations officer, as commander of the 37 aircraft

> formation. The 8/10 to 9/10 cumulus, plus middle clouds, plus smokescreen at the target made it necessary to call again on the PFF [Pathfinder Force] technique. There were strike photos, however, and they showed hits on the north side of the river at Hamburg, a little northeast of the MPI [mean point of impact or target]. There were no enemy aircraft. We lost two Fortresses on the mission to the moderate to intense and extremely accurate flak defending the city.
>
> Levitoff's [pilot] Fortress 297330, "Chug-A-Lug IV," was last seen at 10.54 in the target area, its number-three engine propeller gone after a direct flak hit. The Fortress dropped back and nosed down. Two to five objects were seen coming out of the plane. They disappeared into the clouds. Probabilities are these might have been bailers out, performing delayed jumps. [2 KIA and 7 POW].
>
> Brummett's [pilot] B-17 338114, "No Comment Needed," was last heard of at Noon. Oil was streaming from his number-one engine, and his left wingtip was smoking. Over the VHF the pilot reported he was turning back toward the continent because of a hole in his gas tank. They were last seen under control heading back toward Germany. [9 POW]

When he returned from the mission, Bob discovered that his regular pilot and good friend, Lt. Joe Pearce, was off again for another trip to a flak hotel. The Pearce crew was split up, and suddenly Bob was doing what he had dreaded most, flying with an unfamiliar crew:

> In November, I flew back-to-back missions on two different B-17s, each with a different crew and pilot. Joe was back in the flak hotel, and Duke [Dale Winsor], our regular copilot, was busy flying as first pilot and training new copilots in other bombers. When I looked around that morning [November 9th], there wasn't one guy in the crew who I had flown with before. They probably looked at me the same way because it was obvious that they knew each other. I knew that gunners occasionally had to fill in on other crews, but this was the first time for me. But it also wasn't my first time around the block, so I chatted with them and, once I was down in my turret, just did my job. But I didn't like the feeling of not seeing familiar faces, especially after the previous two tough missions where we had gone through some bad flak. Fortunately, that mission to Oeuvres-Chesney [France] turned out to be a milk run, short and sweet.

The next day Bob flew to Cologne, Germany, with another group of strangers, this time piloted by Lt. John Steinwinter. "I can't tell you how unsettling it can be to be on the intercom and not recognize who is saying what to who," Bob told me. "The crew of a B-17 was a tight-knit little team, and you got to know the other gunners' habits up there. The pilots had their own habits and flying styles as well, their own personalities, routines, and expectations . . . I was lucky that my first twenty-eight missions were with the guys that I had trained with back in the States; I always knew at least six or seven of the crew."

Though once again Bob's bomber made it back to Ridgewell unscathed, the November 10 entry for that mission in the 381st combat diary outlined one of the many ways that you could die in combat:

> We went to Cologne on the tenth, and Col. Leber, with Capt. Watson as his pilot, was again in the lead ship of the 37 aircraft formation. It was 10/10 to 8/10 at the target, and bombing was done by G/H equipment with a Pathfinder assist. Flak was moderate and fairly accurate.
>
> We lost no aircraft, but an unfortunate accident cost us one man: 1Lt. LeRoy Drummond, 535th (bombardier of hell's angel), who was killed, when just after the bombing run, the Fortress flying above Drummond's ship, with three bombs fouled in the bay, suddenly got rid of its load.
>
> Two of the bombs ripped off the nose of Drummond's Fortress and fell clear. The third crashed into the nose compartment and hit Lt. Drummond on the head, killing him instantly. The bomb remained jammed in the floor of the nose for about 45 minutes before it could be dislodged and dropped out of the forward hatch. The rest of the crew, unharmed, were hospitalized upon return to base. They were shocked by the accident to Drummond.

On November 11, the weather over Europe closed in again, and for the next ten days only one mission flew out of Ridgewell. During the downtime, medals were handed out, and Bob sent a letter home telling his folks that he had been awarded the Distinguished Flying Cross.

November 19, 1944, Sunday

Dear Mom and Dad,

I want to say it this time—as you can probably guess, it's still raining.

This morning we were allowed to sleep late so I really sawed logs until it was time to go to church.

Phew wee! I just had a grueling experience—I should get credit for a mission for it. When I returned from church there was a note on my bed saying I was to be at Headquarters dressed in Class A's at 1300 (in 15 minutes!). So I jumped in my blouse and found out that several of us were having our DFC's presented by the Colonel.

So after a Major read a flowery speech, we each in turn had the old brass pinned on. Boy was I nervous. Oh, well, it's over now, and I'll send the medal home soon—enclosed is the award—please let me know when you receive it.

Was reading magazines in the lounge this afternoon early when I noticed a very familiar sight on the front of "AIR FORCE." Yes, it's my old standby, the ball turret on our B-17. The picture is a perfect example of what you could see me doing in the early morning before a mission. He's putting in his guns.

Gosh there isn't much more to talk about today. I haven't heard from the gunnery captain as yet but expect to soon.

Until tomorrow.

Lots of Love to all, Bob

Distinguished Flying Crosses, or DFCs, were awarded to the members of Bob's original crew as follows:

2Lt. Gene Weisser, navigator, October 9, 1944

1Lt. Joseph Pearce, pilot, October 14, 1944

2Lt. Dale (Duke) Winsor, copilot, October 21, 1944

Sgt. Robert Harper, ball turret gunner, November 18, 1944

Sgt. Bentley, radio operator, and Sgt. Charles Bowman, gunner, November 22, 1944 (Bentley and Bowman were MIA on November 22 and received their DFCs when they returned to base)

1Lt. Mort Yolofsky, bombardier, January 2, 1945

Two days after Bob wrote that letter home to his parents, he took off in the B-17 "Colonel Bub" on his fourth mission to the dreaded Luna Oil Works in Merseburg, Germany, where his luck, or at least some of it, would finally run out.

CHAPTER 13
SHOT DOWN!

Mission 31 November 21 Merseburg, Germany 42-38159 "Colonel Bub"

As fuel, chemicals, and lubricants decreased in supply, Germany continued to harden the defenses around their vital chemical plants at Merseburg. More-sophisticated German flak guns arrived, making up for the dwindling supply of protective fighter planes. On November 2, 1944, the 91st BG, flying out of their base in Bassingbourn, sent thirty-seven B-17s against Merseburg, with disastrous results. A third of their planes were shot down, resulting in the loss of 114 crewmen, Merseburg proving once again that it was one of the most dangerous missions in Europe.

It was also hard to tell for the mission planners of the 8th AF when "enough would be enough," and they suspected that the Merseburg plants were continuing to function despite the weekly poundings. According to discovered German documents and interviews that took place after the war, the production records of the Leuna Synthetic Oil Works indicated that despite suffering through a half-dozen punishing bombing raids in the prior two months, the plants were back up to 28 percent capacity by November 20.

By coincidence, on November 21 the 8th Air Force decided to hit this target again. It would turn out to be Bob's fourth and last mission to Merseburg. Bob's experience that day was recorded in three places: in his journal, in a letter from navigator Lt. Gene Weisser, and in a letter home to his parents. Bob and I also talked about his experience several times, and I have drawn from these sources for a complete reimagining of that fateful day:

> When we gathered beneath our B-17 that morning of my fourth mission to Merseburg, I looked around and there were two new gunners plus a new copilot [Bill Pettit] that I had never seen before . . . and Joe was still in the rest home. . . . But at least we had some of the boys back together again, and our regular copilot, Duke Winsor, was in charge that day, piloting the ship . . . Gene Weisser was navigator and Mort Yolofsky was bombardier. We had all been to Merseburg before, so I'm sure we were apprehensive, to say the least.

Everything started out okay; we crossed the Channel in a large formation of bombers stretched out for miles. France was no longer a problem for flak by then, so though we kept a sharp eye for fighters, we could at least relax for the first part of the mission. At 50 miles or so short of Merseburg, some German fighters made a single pass through our formation and managed to take out our number one engine. We weren't that far from Merseburg, so Duke made the call to try to get the bombs on target, and we continued our run in. Nearing Merseburg, I could see a black cloud ahead, which was the flak that was hitting another bomber group that was arriving first.

We would have to fly through that flak for some twenty minutes. It was awful. They would have our range dialed in by the time we got there. I had a bad feeling.

Like I said, the flak around Merseburg was merciless that day, and after we dropped our payload, we were hit a couple more times as we turned away. Two of the remaining three engines were damaged. I think only one of them was still at full power. We soon lost speed and altitude and had to drop out of formation. We all knew what that meant; we had seen what had happened to other bombers that fell behind. We were over Germany, headed south, in the wrong direction, our plane crippled. And all alone . . . we were in big trouble. Really big trouble . . . that much was clear.

They got me up out of the ball turret right away, and I went into the radio room. The tail gunner joined us there. We went off oxygen soon enough; without those big engines firing, the plane was strangely quiet. After a few minutes, Bill Pettit, the copilot, came back to talk to us. He said they weren't sure how far we could get, given the damage. But we had a choice; we could head for Switzerland and try to get her down on the ground, or bail out over neutral territory. Switzerland was still a little closer than England, but we'd be interned there for the rest of the war . . . or we could go for home or at least try to make it past the front lines and either bail out or find a field and try to get the plane down. Our pilots wanted us to vote on it. A couple of the guys were getting close to completing their missions, and they didn't want to be in a POW camp even if it was in Switzerland. They just wanted to go home. There wasn't any time for talk, and less than a minute later the vote went 6–3 to try for England. I voted for England as well. So Duke slowly banked the plane, and we headed for home, trying to avoid the places we knew the Germans had heavy antiaircraft concentrations.

We were sort of gliding, nursing those engines, trying to maintain altitude. The plane had holes in it, but none of us had been wounded. Right away we started trying to lighten her up, trying to preserve our altitude for as long as possible, throwing everything out that we could think of. We wanted to drop my belly turret out as well; it weighed half a ton. But we didn't have the tools along for the job. (It would have taken a socket wrench with an extension and three different sockets to remove thirty bolts, including climbing back down into the ball turret again.) We tossed all the guns and ammunition; the radios went last . . . then we spread out our flak jackets on the radio room floor, and we all went in there and sat on them except the pilots, flight engineer, and the navigator. Occasionally we would take ground fire, especially as we got lower. I thought I could hear flak and bullets hitting the plane. We felt like sitting ducks.

Some time went by; I couldn't tell you now just how long, maybe just an hour or so . . . but Charley Bowman, our top turret gunner and flight engineer, came back to the radio room. "Boys," he shouted, "Duke can't keep her up much longer! Time to go . . . we gotta get out!"

That was it for me! I knew how conservative Charley was, a real serious guy. He went back and released the waist door and jumped. I was right behind him!

Frankly, there was no trauma. I was just tickled to death to get out of that airplane. We had been under ground fire on and off for almost two hours, and any lucky shot to our gas tanks would have blown us out of the sky; I was thrilled to get out! I don't remember pulling the rip cord, but the parachute opened, and I remembered the instructions. We had never practiced jumping, of course; there was no time for that during our training; they needed to get crews over to England to replace the ones that were getting shot down, but they had told us how to pull the rip cord. [Bob laughed] I saw a tall haystack down in a big farm field, and while I was looking up at the chute, pulling on those cords and trying to drift over to this haystack, I hit the ground.

That was probably lucky, because I was relaxed and not stiffened up when I hit the ground. Bit through my tongue, but I was okay. I still had the rip cord's metal handle in my hand. The field where I landed was in a valley, and I couldn't see very far. I didn't know where I was, whether I was in enemy territory or in American-held French territory that we had recaptured. I had my .45 service revolver with me, and we had been told that if you were captured with a gun, the Germans could shoot you. So, I just threw my gun into the haystack and sat down for a few minutes. All of a sudden, I saw men coming over the hill. I didn't know if they were friendly or otherwise. They all gathered around me. I couldn't understand a word they said, but I never shook so many hands in my life. And it turned out they meant me no harm; they were just excited to get hold of the parachute because it was made from silk.

Not much later, an American jeep came roaring into the field to gather me up, and we headed out for the nearest village, just south of the town of Dinant, Belgium, where most of my crew had gathered. Word came in that our navigator, Gene, was in a different location but doing fine, so we had all made it! Other than my bloody tongue and [copilot] Bill Pettit's sprained ankle, we were all in good shape. The guys showed me a map. Turns out, if we had bailed five or ten minutes earlier, we would have wound up prisoners of war. We stayed in the back of a bakery that night. We were told not to go out, because German commandos were still operating behind the lines, and the village was not totally secure. There was some talk about a sniper team out there after dark . . . so, we just huddled in there together and tried to get some sleep that first night. We still had our flight suits, so we were warm enough, though none of us had weapons at that point. . . . It was a quiet night, though in the far distance there was the slightest rumblings. Like thunder. No doubt it was the war, but far, far away . . . artillery.

Bright and early the next day, an Army Engineers officer took us to a really nice little hotel, just a short ride from the bakery but in the small town of Dinant. He told us that the "Colonel Bub" had come down in a nearby field. Some of us went to visit her, expecting to find a wreck. Instead, there she was, standing there in the field, surrounded by townspeople. Somehow, she had landed herself with none of us aboard! People were emptying out the fuel from her in every which way. It looked like some were smoking cigarettes, so I didn't get too close.

In a letter written many years later, the navigator, Lt. Gene Weisser, would also tell the story of that fateful day and add another element to it. Unbeknown to Bob and the other gunners braced in the radio room, disconnected from the intercom as they were and with no view of what was going on outside, two P-51s had shown up to fend off any German fighters that might be looking for an easy prey. After stating that many of the details of that day were now cloudy, Gene did have some distinct memories forty years later of the day that he wanted to share:

> My parachute saved my life twice that day. It was my 34th mission, and we were headed for Merseburg, a long haul. We got hit going in and got hit bad over the bomb run and had to drop out of formation because we were gradually losing altitude. Finding our way back out of enemy territory alone called for some tricky navigation to make sure we avoided antiaircraft gun installations that were shown on the map.
>
> Enemy aircraft was still a worry, so we called for fighter escort and two P-51s answered and remained on our wing till we got into friendly territory. I always wished I could have been able to thank those guys for risking their necks for us. Our rate of descent was too rapid to get to the English Channel, so Dale [pilot Dale Winsor] decided to find some open ground to bring the B-17 down. But eventually, because of the nature of the damage, he gave the order that we were all to bail out. He would be the last man out after he put the ship on automatic pilot to descend in a circular pattern.
>
> Leaving the plane was easy. The bomb bay doors were open or at least partly open, and all we had to do was straddle them, then pull our legs together. I will never forget the sensation. One minute I was surrounded by noise in the Fortress, then the next minute was suddenly quiet, with just the wind. I counted, then pulled the rip cord, and the chute opened beautifully and I was drifting down, I thought slowly, toward an open field. It was a wonderful feeling, and I was enjoying it but remembered that we were taught to check the wind direction so we could land with the wind at our back to prevent the chute from dragging us off-balance when we hit the ground. I got so engrossed in this effort that I hit the ground before I knew it and just collapsed onto the ground like a big ball, and the chute dropped right beside me. That had to be the hand of Providence because I had no injuries from the landing.
>
> I picked myself up and I could see a man running toward me. As he got closer, I could see that he had a pitchfork in his hand. When he got close enough, he started talking to me excitedly in French [fortunately, Gene spoke rudimentary French]. I told him I was an American and finally convinced him that he had nothing to fear, and

that all I wanted was to find the nearest US Military Group in the area. He helped me with the parachute and asked what I was going to do with it. He said he would be glad to take it because his wife could make many things from it. I told him it was his, and we were best friends from that moment on. He eventually got me to a Corps of Engineers group in the town of Dinant, Belgium, and I was reunited with most of my crew there the next day.

Interestingly enough, once we were all out of the plane, our B-17 on autopilot slowly descended in circles and landed itself with very little damage. Later on, some of the guys went and visited her to retrieve a few important things they'd left behind. What an amazing sight in that farm field; the B-17 had survived on her own!

We stayed with the Corps of Engineers for three days, and they were very good to us. They helped us recuperate from our harrowing experience. I returned to Ridgewell on November 25th and flew my last mission on December 4th. Really sweated that one out.

During my research, I discovered a photo of the "Colonel Bub" sitting in that field, its numbers, 42-38159, still clearly visible on its tail. I had come across many accounts of B-17s making it back to base and landing successfully after being literally shot apart and with large pieces missing, but this was the only time that I heard of a B-17 landing without a crew on board. The Sperry autopilot that guided the empty plane to its unmanned landing was a primitive computer by today's standards but did the job perfectly!

When the 381st combat diary updated its November 21 entry, they didn't have much to say about the "Colonel Bub's" adventure or its missing crew. They simply mentioned that a Fortress had gone down, and noted the fate of the copilot but not of the other crew members. Though the "Colonel Bub's" miraculous landing sans crew surely deserved its own entry, by the time the crew made it back to base it was already old news:

> There was no flak at Friedberg, but there was plenty of it at the primary [Merseburg]. It was intense and accurate, and it gave rise to a crop of wounds and forced one of our aircraft to crash-land in Brussels. 2Lt. William G. Pettit, 533rd co-pilot, who was in the aircraft that landed away from base, suffered a sprained left ankle when he parachuted from the Fortress. His 'chute had been damaged by flak and refused to open; he had to rip it apart in the air and it just opened in time to prevent more serious injury when he hit the ground.

On November 23, two days after parachuting to safety, Bob and the crew of the "Colonel Bub" were treated to a Thanksgiving meal in Dinant, Belgium, by the Army Engineers. I can't improve on the heartwarming letter that Bob sent his parents almost eighty years ago that describes that Thanksgiving. You will note that he omits most of the details of the mission in that letter, like a good son sparing his parents any more worry than they were already experiencing:

11-27-44 England

Dear Mom and Dad,

My but it's good to be back in the hut again. A lot has happened this past week as you probably know by the V-Mail I just wrote. We had a pretty bad time over Germany last week, but we all made it back to Belgium. We all had to bail out.

Duke was our pilot, and he did a wonderful job and really saved all of us. It was quite an experience to jump, and I often wondered how it would go if it ever came to that. Now I know and it is really OK. I came down next to a haystack that I tried to hit, and the only injury I got was a sore tongue that I bit. All the others are okay, too.

The Belgium people came over every hill around me, and I had to shake about 100 hands. I was so glad I was in friendly territory. I wasn't sure when we left the plane. I didn't understand a word but managed to communicate well with motions, etc. I gave them my chute after saving enough of it to make myself a scarf. An Army Engineer picked me up within an hour, and we [the crew] were all together again in a little town.

We stayed several days with the engineers in a fine hotel and made some lasting friends. Boy! The fellows were nice to us—a swell bunch of boys. . . . I picked up some souvenirs, Mom, which I will send home (wooden shoes, brass figurines, which the town is noted for). Gosh there is a lot I want to tell you about my travels. Hmmm. More to talk about when I get home.

We each bought back a bottle of champagne for the fellows who packed our chutes. They were really tickled to get them.

We had turkey after all for Thanksgiving at the hotel. Boy! I was never so thankful for anything in my life. Just to be around. It was more than just luck that brought us back.

I just took my first shower in a week. I got my clothes and stuff and junk back out of supply. (They pick up your stuff when you're missing.) What a wonderful shower, too.

Mom, I sent a cablegram to let you know that I was OK because they said that you may have been sent a cable that I was MIA [missing in action]. I hope they didn't send you one because they are so deceiving. Even when you are a prisoner of war, you're [the family] kept in the dark for so long before the time you receive MIA [status].

Well, enough for now; I am really sleepy so I will just hit my good old sack again. We have only four (missions) to go now so we should be done by Christmas.

Surely thinking of you all. So glad to be back.

All my love, Bob

Crew of the "Colonel Bub" on the November 21 mission to Merseburg:

Dale (Duke) Winsor	pilot
Bill Pettit	copilot
Gene Weisser	navigator
Mort Yolofsky	bombardier
Bruce Bentley	radio operator
Charles Bowman	top turret gunner
Everett Coats	right waist gunner
Bob Harperball	turret gunner
Dan Adair	tail gunner

The "Colonel Bub" would be repaired and returned to England for combat. But on January 21, 1945, just sixty days after her first forced landing, the "Colonel Bub" would force-land a second time on the Continent, this time with her crew on board. Uninjured, all nine men of the crew would return safely to base several days later. However, the damage from this "wheels-up landing" would be so severe that "Colonel Bub" would be left in that farm field until it could be scrapped and salvaged in place at war's end.

CHAPTER 14
PILOT JOE PEARCE

Joe Pearce's nephew, Robert Pearce, recalls the following:

> My Uncle Joe [pilot 1Lt. Joe Pearce] told me a little story about the war and his time at Ridgewell that really stuck in my mind. It was the middle of Uncle Joe's tour and he had been flying a lot, not only taking up his own crew but occasionally training a new crew, flying in the first seat [pilot's seat]. He was pretty exhausted. One morning Uncle Joe was piloting a B-17, taxiing towards the runway for takeoff, on yet another combat mission. In an adjacent field he noticed a man driving a tractor, plowing a long furrow in the distance. He grew mesmerized by the sight, wishing they could trade places for just one day. Their mission that day turned out to be a particularly tough one, a long run into Germany. They landed back at Ridgewell in their shot-up B-17 just as the sun was sinking in the sky. As they taxied towards their hardstand to park their wounded bomber, Uncle Joe looked out and there was that same farmer, still plowing the same field, but closer now. He remembered thinking, we couldn't have more different lives, we couldn't have spent our day any more differently than the two of us just had.

Pilot Joe Pearce figured heavily in Bob Harper's story of his time in the 8th Army Air Force. Not only did Bob train with Joe in Florida, but they would also fly twenty-seven combat missions together, including their first and last missions. According to Bob, "Joe Pearce is the reason I made it through the war in one piece, the steadiest hand and the calmest man in a fight that you could hope for at the controls of your B-17." Bob and I agreed that Joe deserved a chapter of his own.

Like many who served in World War II, Joe Pearce traveled his own route to become a pilot in the 8th Air Force. As a student at Milford High School, he was a fine athlete and lettered in basketball, graduating with the Class of '37, then working for the post office for a while before entering the University of Pennsylvania. After a year of college, Joe dropped out and enlisted as a private in the Army and trained as a radio operator. When given the chance, he transferred to aviation cadet training at Freeman Army Airfield, winning his wings and commission on November 3, 1943. After a short leave, he was sent along to MacDill Field in Florida, where he would hook up with Bob and the rest of the crew for months of crew training before heading to England in May 1944 to join the 381st Bomb Group.

On August 3, 1944, after just five weeks in combat and with fourteen successful missions already under his belt, Joe Pearce was promoted to first lieutenant and deemed ready to break in new pilots. Four days later, Joe Pearce and his crew would do just that with a new copilot aboard, Lt. Rich Ellis. Lt. Ellis's humorous recounting of this first combat mission would later be captured in a book, *On Final Approach*, written by another 381st pilot, Edward C. Carr. The story takes place aboard the B-17 "Honey," with Bob Harper down in the ball turret and Lt. Joe Pearce in the pilot seat:

Rich's First Mission

It was standard procedure when a new crew arrived at the 381st Bomb Group, both the pilot and co-pilot would fly their first few missions as a co-pilot with an experienced combat pilot. After a couple of missions under their belts, they would return to fly with their original crew. A few years ago, Ellis Richard (Rich), our crew's co-pilot, sketched out the story of his very first mission and sent the rough draft to me:

These are the memories of my first mission. My crew arrived at the base (Ridgewell) on August 7, 1944, and we were happy to learn that the monthly party was on for that evening. Some welcome!

About four o'clock the next morning an orderly shook me and remarked cheerfully that I was flying with Lieutenant Pearce. I politely informed him that this was obviously a mistake as I had just arrived. For some reason this seemed to amuse him, and he repeated his original statement.

So, I staggered in the dark to the mess and the briefing room and someone shoved me into a truck that eventually dumped me into Lieutenant Pearce's lap. He cheerfully informed me that we were flying left low box (or some such thing—I'm no longer sure of the nomenclature), for which reason he would be sitting in the co-pilot seat. I was too groggy to argue the point, besides which I was sure that he could certainly fly the plane from either side.

But when he cheerfully informed me, as I taxied along, that I would be taking off from the short runway, my stomach told me to give further thought to my situation. I knew something that Lieutenant Pearce did not: at Operational Training Unit the co-pilot was just a passenger until the last week when he received flight training at the controls of a B-17. My secret was that my pilot Ed Carr chose that time to be grounded with an ear infection which in turn grounded the entire crew. This made for great sack time but didn't advance my skill as a pilot. Finally, an instructor took me up and checked me out after three takeoffs and three landings. (He didn't appear to be too interested in my welfare.)

As our take-off moment neared, I took the philosophical viewpoint that you only die once, stomped on the brakes, gave her full throttle, and let her rip. Much to my surprise we cleared the fence at the end of the runway and headed out.

The mission that day was to Caen in support—at 14,000 feet—of our ground troops who were trying to break loose. It was a beautiful clear day and every direction I looked, the sky was filled with little groups of our bombers encircled by friendly fighters. To avoid dropping bombs on our own troops, no bombs were to be dropped short of a radio beacon that was directed across our flight path. Some distance from the target site, the enemy 88s were turned loose on us. The first several bursts of flak alongside our plane fascinated me. It was as though some unseen giant was blowing smoke rings at us. Everywhere I looked was the same. It appeared that each group of our planes had contracted with its own assigned 88s to lay down a path of black top and I recalled a remark by an experienced airman at an orientation lecture that "the flak was so thick we let down our landing gear and taxied across it." An understatement, I decided. In addition to the bursts of flak alongside, frequent lurches of the plane kept us informed of the near bursts below the fuselage. I began to feel like a duck flying across the Colusa Gun Club marshes. Fear gripped my heart. It was only a matter of time until we would take a direct hit.

Finally, we dropped our load and headed for the friendly skies of home. But my terror wasn't quite over. There was still the little matter of landing back at Ridgewell. So, I cheerfully dropped the plane in (as I had for my practice landings at Dyersburg and more subsequent landings at Ridgewell). Lieutenant Pierce cheerfully remarked, "Good. I like a solid landing that stays put."

The 381st lost no planes that day, but every plane on the mission received more or less serious flak damage, resulting in a stand down that following day and more sack time.

Bob was in the belly turret that day with an up-close view of the flak, while "frequent lurches of the plane kept us informed of the near burst below the fuselage." For the next five missions, Lt. Ellis would fly in the copilot seat with the Pearce crew, gaining valuable experience, while their regular copilot, Dale Winsor, got his chance to serve as senior pilot aboard other B-17s.

Though Bob and Joe became good friends during their time at Ridgewell, Bob was not aware that Lt. Pearce was flying more than he was. In July, in addition to the scrubbed mission and the thirteen combat missions that Bob flew with him, Pearce put in six training missions. In September, while Bob and the rest of their crew were waiting for their trip to the Flak hotel, Joe piloted long back-to-back missions to Germany on September 6 and 7, leading other crews. Though Joe would head out with Bob and the crew for that well-deserved rest in Southport in September, it wouldn't be enough. By the time that Bob got to his twenty-fifth mission on October 14, Joe was already on his twenty-ninth, and those extra four missions had taken their toll:

> I guess I never understood how stressful the job of B-17 pilot was until I had some conversations after the war. The pilot and copilot would take turns flying our B-17, fifteen minutes on, fifteen minutes off, switching back and forth. The pilot had primary responsibility in emergencies; I'm sure that's why they put him in the left seat, so he could use his strong right arm. It was physically exhausting for both pilots, and the mental strain was incredible as they steered us into those walls of flak. One wrong decision could also send us into another B-17 laden down with fuel and bombs, and no one survived those collisions . . . and the weather, fog, and heavy clouds . . . I can't emphasize how close together the planes were, or the feeling when we came out of a cloud roaring along at 180 mph and suddenly found ourselves close enough to *spit and hit* our wingman . . . I would keep my eyes peeled and spin that ball turret 360 degrees. . . . Well, we all kept our eyes peeled for good reason . . . we saw a few accidents and we had our own close calls up there in the clouds . . . November was a tough month all around, and I missed having Joe there.

The authors of *Masters of the Air* probably put the bomber pilot's dilemma best:

> If fighter pilots lived in a world of split seconds, bomber boys lived in one of agonizing hours, with too much time to think about their own end, which depended inordinately on lady fortune. In its testing and

> training programs the Air Force looked for different qualities in fighter and bomber pilots: physical strength, judgment, emotional stamina, dependability, teamplay, discipline and leadership in bomber pilots . . . rapid hand-eye coordination, aggressiveness, boldness, individuality, and a zest for battle in fighter pilots. In a profile of an ideal bomber pilot, the Air Force noted: "The attitude of the crew members was that they would gladly let some other crew have the hottest pilot in the group if they could have the man who, when in a tough spot, where a decision might mean life or death to them had to be made, would quickly . . . make the best possible decision." For bomber pilots, "intellectual traits were more highly prized than sensory-motor skills. "Love of blood sports, cockiness . . . and lack of high intellectual stature would prove to be qualifying factors for fighter pilots," said the Air Force Study.
>
> But bomber pilots suffered much-higher casualties than fighter pilots, and with greater responsibilities as crew commanders, they were more susceptible to mental breakdowns or combat fatigue. "The task of fighter pilot is ideal for high motivation, Air Force psychologists concluded. Fighter pilots had shorter, more-informal briefings, five minutes to the bomber crews' one hour. They took off and formed much more quickly and less dangerously than bomber pilots and, unless they were strafing, were rarely the targets of Nazi flak gunners. . . . A Fortress crew had to sit and take it, like a crew of a submarine under assault and trapped on the floor of the ocean.

The 381st Bomb Group was served by the 242nd Medical Attachment, and while combat fatigue was nothing to joke about, this lighthearted entry by Maj. Gaillard in the 242nd's journal says a lot about the stress that these young pilots were under:

> Captain J.F. has been sweating out his missions to a marked degree, having battle dreams, talking in his sleep, and having considerable mental disturbances. The boys in his barracks say he flies his ship from the time his sleeping begins until he awakens again. The other night the men went into the barracks and found Captain J.F. flying a tough mission. Apparently, his ship was hit and he exclaimed, "Co-pilot, feather number four . . . Co-pilot, what is your name?" Lieutenant P., sleeping nearby, answered him back in his sleep. Then both men, while still sound asleep (but talking to each other) piloted the severely damaged Fort back to the base safely.

On October 14, Lt. Joe Pearce was awarded the Distinguished Flying Cross "for extraordinary achievement in aerial combat." Following the award, Joe would get a few weeks off from combat and then head off to a flak hotel for a while longer until he returned to service and was flying combat again missions with the 533rd Squadron on November 26.

The men of his crew were glad to get him back. After the war, they all credited Joe as the main reason they made it back home alive. At a 381st BG reunion, navigator Gene Weisser would tell Joe's nephew Robert this:

> We all agreed that Joe was the perfect leader for our crew. He was calm no matter what was happening all around us. His voice on the intercom was as cool as a cucumber, and this demeanor was contagious. He spent more time checking out his B-17 before taking it up for combat than any other pilot I flew with. . . . I will always be proud to have been part of that great crew. I feel I am alive today because God gave me the best pilot in the USAF, Joe Pearce, and one of the most rugged aircraft in World War II, the B-17G. Enough said.

On November 26, while Bob and his crew were still making their way back to England after parachuting to safety over Belgium, Lt. Pearce was flying again, this time on a mission attacking a railroad viaduct in the Ruhr Valley. On the twenty-ninth, he piloted a mission to hit the oil storage in Zeitz. The following day, he flew once again to the "Flak Hell Leuna Works" at Merseburg, where Bob and his crew had just been shot down the previous week. On December 9, Lt. Pearce was along when the 381st BG commander, Col. Leber, flying in a 533rd Squadron B-17, led the formation against railroad marshaling yards in Stuttgart. The flak was heavy and accurate, and five of their bombers were badly damaged, though they all managed to limp back to base.

After flying those four missions in fifteen days, Lt. Pearce had a week off. Then, on December 18, he led the remnants of his old Florida crew on a mission to Cologne, Germany. The Battle of the Bulge was underway, and the expected milk run quickly devolved into a close call for the crew of B-17 43-37791. It would require flying two different B-17s on the same mission, but once again the steady hand of senior pilot Joe Pearce would bring his crew home to safety.

Up next, Joe and Bob reunite for their last month of combat and wind up on the doorstep of the Battle of the Bulge.

CHAPTER 15
HERE WE GO AGAIN! THE BATTLE OF THE BULGE

Mission 32	December 4	Soest	42-97589	unnamed B-17
Mission 33	December 11	Mannheim	42-97059	"Marsha Sue"
Mission 34	December 18	Cologne	43-37791	unnamed B-17
Mission 35	December 28	Remagen	43-38983	"Fort Lansing Emancipator"

Bob Harper:

> I am not sure what we expected when we got back to base after getting shot down over Merseburg, but they didn't make much of a fuss over us when we returned. Just put us back into the combat schedule after a couple of days off. Of course, none of us had any idea that a German counteroffensive known as the Battle of the Bulge was about to unfold. And that somehow my new crew would wind up on the ground not far from the German advance!

During December, German fighters were once again mostly absent from the sky, though as I wrote earlier, it was still the luck of the draw for squadrons flying combat missions into Germany. On the other hand, whenever the weather allowed, the numbers of Allied bombers in those same skies continued to grow. A combat report from the 381st BG combat diary on Bob's thirty-third mission tells the story:

> December 11, 1944. Ten squadrons of bombers took part in today's attack on a railroad bridge spanning the river between Ludwigshafen and Mannheim. On takeoff at 06.30 hours the weather was clear, damp, and cold. There were 1,600 heavy bombers over Germany today, the largest number to attack the Reich in one day. The majority attacked targets in the Ruhr Valley. The 381st formation found a 10/10th cloud cover at the target, and bombing was carried out by instruments. Flak was meagre but accurate; no enemy fighters were seen, but a 532nd ship was lost in action.

In hindsight the lack of German fighter planes during those first two weeks of December would be easily explained; the Germans were saving them for their big surprise attack. On December 16, the German army executed its last major ground offense of the war, launching a surprise attack through the dense forests of the Ardennes region between Belgium and Luxembourg, hoping to reach the Belgian port of Antwerp while dividing the Allied forces in two. At first the foul weather cooperated with the German offensive, keeping the overwhelming air superiority of the Allied powers out of the mix and cutting reconnaissance to a minimum. Two days after the "Battle of the Bulge" began, the Allied forces still didn't know that almost 600,000 German soldiers and over a thousand tanks were on the move. And two thousand German aircraft that they had been "saving" for this last counteroffensive were in hiding, waiting for an opportunity to support the German advance!

When dawn broke on December 18, Bob found himself standing under the belly of B-17 43-37791. It was just a routine day for him, another mission to tick off the list. It would be this one and then just one more, and he would finally be done with his combat service. After installing their guns, the crew waited for the officers to arrive. Bob joked with Bruce Bentley and Charlie Bowman, crewmates since Florida. The other two gunners, Charles Brown and Tony Ferrara, were new to him. When the officers finally showed up, there were new faces there as well. Copilot Dale Winsor, bombardier Mort Yolofsky, and navigator Gene Weisser all were missing, having completed their thirty-fifth mission three days prior. But Bob was relieved to see that his pilot for the mission was the man he trusted the most, 1Lt. Joe Pearce.

Of the over nine hundred 8th Air Force bombers that were sent out that day, half of them returned due to the bad weather, the same bad weather that was allowing the German army to continue to advance undetected in the Ardennes. But the target that day for the 381st BG was the railroad marshaling yards of Cologne, and the flight was deemed doable. Though they didn't see any fighters going in, Bob's B-17 took some of the "very light flak" that was later reported. Within minutes of unloading their bombs, their B-17 developed a runaway prop. Harper remembers:

> One of our engines was gone, and Joe started decreasing altitude pretty quickly and we left the formation. There were no fighters around, so I got called out of the ball turret and joined Bruce in the radio room. We spread out some flak jackets on the floor. As we got lower and lower, the other gunners joined us and took crash positions. We suspected that any German down there with a gun would be firing at us. Joe was

looking for friendly territory to set us down, but we were still in the heavy clouds . . . once again he did a great job of getting us down on the ground . . . I seem to remember, though, that the fuselage cracked just past the radio spar. That the landing left it unflyable.

Pilot Joe Pearce would also share his memory of that day with his nephew Robert:

Uncle Joe told me that they had a runaway prop not long after they turned for home. A runaway prop results in an engine overspeed and can cause an engine to catch fire or even disintegrate, resulting in a catastrophe, spreading engine parts through the fuselage like a direct hit from an "88." Uncle Joe immediately started looking around for somewhere to land, but it was hard to figure out where they were in relationship to the front lines. The weather was cloudy with very low visibility. They finally got below the clouds and headed over German lines, taking some ground fire. Eventually he couldn't risk it any longer and decided to make an emergency landing at the first airfield they came to.

They were not sure where the current battle lines were located, but they had to set it down on the ground as quickly as possible or risk the engine blowing and taking the ship with her. They saw a small airstrip and decided to give it a go. They came in hard and managed to stop by the end of the runway. It turned out that they had landed safely behind the Allied lines near Ghent, Belgium, at a small forward fighter base. The base had no maintenance facilities for bombers; it was serving as a fuel and rearm station for the fighters. Uncle Joe didn't remember the outfit but recalls that there was a unit of Polish fighter pilots stationed there who had been serving in England since the war's outbreak.

Uncle Joe said that an Army sergeant informed him that there was no way out of there at the moment but that they could put the crew up until transportation back to England could be arranged. But that it probably wouldn't be for a while. Joe would be given "food chits" each morning that would allow his crew to mess with the fighter crews. So, the nine of them took unused rooms in the barracks and settled in. Then Joe sat the crew down and gave them the skinny. They all agreed that they were in a pretty good situation. They were legitimately stranded and unable to fly back to their base. It might not be a bad place to just wait out the war for a few days. They didn't have any toiletries or change of clothes, but no one had been injured and they were all safely behind the Allied lines.

Bob remembers eating with the fighter pilots that were stationed there:

> Those pilots were really gung ho. They just lived for the fight. And they couldn't wait to get back up in the air. They were complaining about the lack of German fighters during the previous few weeks. I think we told them to stick with us, because we never seemed to have any problem finding them . . . we had a great time talking to them over meals. They had plenty of stories . . . and I guess by then, we had ours as well.

But the crew's short respite didn't last. According to Robert Pearce, a couple of mornings after they landed, his Uncle Joe went to get their food authorization slips, but this time the sergeant had some news:

> Sorry, Sir. But after your men breakfast, they need to report to the armory and draw their weapons.
>
> Uncle Joe tried to correct him. "No, I think you're mistaken, sergeant; we're the aircrew that flew in on that damaged B-17 that's sitting out there."
>
> But the sergeant was adamant. "Sorry, sir, we know who you are, but there's been a breakthrough and the Germans are coming this way, and we need you to check out your weapons. Everyone is going to the front: clerks, cooks, and bottle washers . . . the lot of us."
>
> Joe didn't argue with the sergeant. Back at the barracks, the crew huddled together and discussed their options. Joe had heard that there was another B-17 down not far away, at another small air base. The men were all for getting back to England; it had been months since they fired anything but their big .50-caliber guns. And it had been over a year since their basic training. If the Germans were coming, then as a highly trained B-17 crew they needed to be up in the air bombing them, slowing them down . . . not standing around in a trench somewhere playing infantry. Joe took a few of the men to inspect the other plane. They had all been around B-17s

now for many months and felt confident they could get that one going again. They returned to the fighter base and got a few parts from their own downed B-17, then commandeered a truck, and the whole crew headed back for the other abandoned B-17.

Using the salvaged parts, they made a few simple repairs and got the engines working again. Then they stripped out all the unnecessary equipment, ammo, guns, and anything that wasn't welded down, to lighten her up. They even managed to drop the ball turret out. According to Joe, "he never got the B-17 up very high or flew her very fast, but it was a smooth flight home, taking less than two hours." Though no doubt command at Ridgewell were surprised to see us come back with a different B-17 than we had flown out with, they knew we were okay, and though we had been missing for three or four days, this time they didn't send out MIA notices to our families.

Shot down over Merseburg and then forced-landed on the Continent three weeks later, Bob was still expected to finish up his thirty-five missions. So, on December 28, exactly six months after his first combat mission, he climbed aboard B-17 44-8983, known as the "Fort Lansing Emancipator," and headed out for Remagen, Germany. The same crew that had gone down with him ten days prior was reassembled, with Joe Pearce serving again as pilot; Nelson Schein, copilot; Wilber Stolz, navigator; Bob Lane, bombardier; Bruce Bentley, radio operator; Charles Bowman, top turret gunner; Charles Brown, waist gunner; Bob Harper, belly turret gunner; and Tony Ferrara, tail gunner. This is how Bob remembers his last combat mission:

Funny, our previous flight with that runaway prop could have ended in disaster . . . and now the same nine of us were up in the air again headed for Germany, and these new guys were no longer new guys to me. We had made it through something together, that forced landing back in Belgium They all knew it was Joe's and my last flight, our last mission.

This mission turned out to be what we called a "milk run." There were no fighters and only light flak over the target. We prayed all the way back to Ridgewell that nothing bizarre would happen. When we landed, Joe called me up to the front of the plane and said, "Shorty, turn these engines off."

I still get choked up when I think of that moment. Joe and I were the only two of our original crew to finish together on that particular day. The others had already gone or would be done in a week or so. We all made it somehow. I really don't know how we survived it all . . . Joe looked at me and we just smiled; I think we were both pretty amazed. It was going to take awhile to sink in.

Anyway, we went to our final debriefing and had our usual shot of whiskey. The colonel and the rest of the officers were all there to congratulate us, as they knew we had just finished our thirty-fifth mission. A week later, Joe, me, and a few of the guys all went to London for three days. I think it was the first time in London that I was really relaxed.

Bob's letter home written on New Year's Eve, three days after his final mission, sums it all up:

December 31, 1944

Dear Mom and Dad,

Here it is New Year's Eve, and I was given my only wish, that is to be finished. All I hope now is that you have all received my cablegram telling you the good news. My New Year's Eve present to you! I've just been taking it easy since I've finished—not letter writing—no nothing. Oh, Happy Day! I walked around in a daze after I finished, and it is just today that I'm returning to happy normal life.

Gosh when I look back on what we've been thru—it's hard to believe. Today I wrapped two packages, which are now on the way home.

I'm awaiting my orders to leave the field now. They should come any day. This morning after church I cleaned the house, giving away all my accumulated games, books, etc. to the boys.

Bentley finished today, which makes six of old Pearce's crew that fooled old Jerry. Charley Bowman still has two left.

One of my biggest thrills in finishing was when we crossed the Rhine River for the last time and I saw the swastika for the last time. Boy what a feeling. Then we landed and I put my two feet on good old mother earth.

Well, there isn't much more to talk about, Folks. About all I do now is think of you all and of home and the day that I will get out of the taxi in front of 4146. How about that?

I hope to be home for both birthdays. I should hit it just right.

The boys are pulling my coat tails, so I'll sign off for now. We're going to have a beer or two at "Ye Old Pub" as our New Year's Eve.

Hope all is swell at home. Hello to Joe & Grandma & Grandpa.

All my love, Bob

A FINAL NOTE ON THE BATTLE OF THE BULGE

Four of Bob's missions were to the synthetic fuel plants at Merseburg, part of the big "Oil War" campaign of the summer and fall of 1944. After the war ended, there was an interesting footnote written to the Battle of the Bulge, on the basis of discovered German documents: The newest and most powerful German tank, the Tiger II, had been used to spearhead this German attack. The Tiger II also consumed 2 US gallons of fuel per mile, and the Germans had enough fuel for them (thanks to the Allied oil campaign) for only an estimated 90 miles or so, nowhere near enough to reach Antwerp. Thanks to Bob's four missions to Merseburg and the other fourteen Merseburg missions flown by thousands of brave Allied airmen, at a cost of over 150 B-17s and the lives of over 1,200 airmen, the German panzers literally ran out of gas during the Battle of the Bulge.

The 8th Air Force had punched a giant hole in the German gas tank with their raids. When the weather cleared after Christmas, the crews of the 8th Air Force went back to work pummeling the retreating Germans. Five painful months of war in Europe still awaited all the participants and bystanders (civilians as well), but when Bob finished his thirty-fifth mission on December 28, 1944, the end of the war was finally in sight.

CHAPTER 16
AND THEN THERE WERE NONE

Bob Harper:

> Charlie Bowman left for home today. I'm the last one here now of our old crew. But how happy we all were that we came through so well.

On January 1, 1945, just four days after Bob completed his thirty-fifth mission, the 381st Bomber Group sent thirty-seven bombers to Kassel, Germany. Two of their B-17s were lost to flak, and half of the formation returned battle-damaged. Making the start of the year more difficult, the weather proved to be terrible for flying, with blowing snow and heavy clouds canceling a handful of missions. Though Germany was failing to put up many fighters, on January 21 the 381st BG lost another two bombers due to a tragic midair collision that killed all eighteen airmen. From the 381st BG's combat diary:

> There was no enemy opposition at all, not even flak. Returning to base in haze and high wind, the formation suffered a tragic accident. Two aircraft collided in the traffic pattern and every member of the two crews was killed. Exact details of the accident will never be known. There were those, however, who said they saw a P-47 enter the traffic pattern and cause one of the Fortresses to wing up sharply. One of the Fortresses was seen to cut the tail from the other. None of the crew members had a chance except for Sgt. M. Swartz, tail gunner, who was alive when he was picked up. He died very shortly thereafter, however, in the hospital.

Several other 381st B-17s were shot down during January, and there was an increased number of forced landings on the Continent as well. So much for "things winding down," thought the airmen of the 381st who were still working on completing their thirty-five missions. To add to the continued tension on the base, the crews were made aware that the Germans had added new Messerschmitt Me 262 jets to the skies, with an attacking speed of over 500 mph and the ability to climb above the bombers to an altitude of 37,000 feet.

Despite continued casualties in January, the number of milk runs for the 381st was also on the rise, and by the end of January the airmen flying over a clearly devastated Germany sensed that the war was rapidly drawing to an end. For those who had already completed their combat and were waiting for their ticket home, life took on a new rhythm. Bob stayed busy training new gunners and was sympathetic to their plight, having sweated out his own thirty-five missions.

In a letter home to his parents, Bob painted a happy picture of his new life at Ridgewell.

January 10, 1945

Dear Mom and Dad,

More good news. Both pairs of gloves arrived today along with another great pocket entertainer. Both pairs of gloves fit perfectly, especially the swell leather ones, which are almost too classy to wear. They'll be my new dress gloves.

I haven't any classes today [Bob was now a gunnery instructor] so I'm enjoying our comfortable hut and nice warm stove while I write out a few letters. It's still pretty cold here and snow falls daily. And the streets are fit for ice skates . . .

Dad, I'm certainly thrilled about your trip to Altoona as it sounds like business is looking good in the future. Surely hope so, Dad, as you surely deserve it. And too, you'll NEED additional funds when your wandering son comes home and starts his usual drain on the budget! HO! HO!

It's funny, I have had no desire to leave the base since I finished flying, and I'm not going to until it's time to come home. I have a lot of fun here with the swell bunch of boys in our Hut. Also traveling on these trains is so slow, especially in this cold weather. Well, I'm very content here to wait until it's time to come home.

Charlie Bowman left for home today. I'm the last one here now of our old crew. But how happy we all were that we came thru so well.

Mom, I hope I didn't alarm you too much by writing about our accident (force-landing) and jump (Merseburg). But really, I feel so much better if you all know what goes on here instead of keeping you in the dark like so many other guys do. I hope my V-mail arrived in a week (saying I was finished) and understand they do (get there that quickly). I didn't want to wire you because I know that getting a wire is so alarming before you can read them.

Please tell Joe [Bob's brother] how much I enjoyed his X-mas card. It surely was swell. I just wrote him a letter and enclosed several photos. The photo laboratory at the field here gave me 12 pictures of similar views when I finished my last mission.

The Santa Claus you made is certainly cute and is now hanging from my calendar

The boys in my hut are doing fine (the new crew). They already have 15 missions. Man, I surely sweat them out. (Worry about them when they are flying.)

Well, there isn't much more to say for now except I am counting the days until I see you all again. Hello to Grandpa and Grandma.

All my Love, Bob

In a long entry in his journal, Bob Harper recalls those days on the base while he waited to be sent home:

Well, it was the New Year, 1945, and the shooting war was finally over for me. Back at the base I was given the option of going home and being reassigned or staying on at Ridgewell as a gunnery instructor. I knew that most of the crews, after a 30-day rest in the States, were sent back to the ETO [European theater of operations] or sent to the Pacific to fly B-29s. At that time, I knew I wasn't in very good shape to fly anymore, so I opted to stay and try to help the new crews coming in.

So, I was assigned to instructing new gunnery crews about the ball turret. Passing along to them any tips I might have gained in my six months of combat and answering any questions that they put to me. The war was still going on all around us, and though the German Air Force was pretty much gone by January, they were still getting up there on occasion, including some of those new Nazi jet fighters. And of course, flak was still taking down some of our B-17s. So, it was still a very serious business . . .

When I finally left our base at Great Yeldum, I was assigned, as were the majority of flight crews, to return on the famous ocean liner the *Queen Elizabeth*. It had been converted to a hospital ship, and those of us who were non-commissioned officers, I was a Staff Sergeant, were asked to load the casualties. It was a traumatic experience—to say the least.

Most of the soldiers were from Patton's army and other infantry divisions fighting in Germany. There were a few airmen mixed in as well. Being small (I think I was back down to 110 pounds or less), it became quite a chore loading stretchers all day. But we could really feel for these men, many of whom took their injuries lightly even though they had lost an arm or leg . . . or both. If there is any humor in this, it is that I looked for men with a thin face, hoping for a light stretcher to carry on the ship. But most of them were all heavily cast, so that added to the weight. We were worn out after four days of filling up the ship with casualties . . . mostly mentally (exhausted) from seeing those poor guys. An experience that I will never forget . . .

The *Queen* was huge, and mostly you didn't realize you were at sea. I remember one day I watched our wake as we zigzagged in an attempt to confuse the U-boats which were still active in the Atlantic. We were told that another thing in our favor was that this was the fastest ocean liner at that time, traveling at some 32 knots. (During her war service as a troopship, *Queen Elizabeth* carried more than 750,000 troops while sailing some 500,000 miles.)

"We reached New York in five days and were immediately flown to an air base in Santa Anna, California, which was a combination rehabilitation and reassignment center. What a resort! They wanted to fatten us up, so lots of great meals and relaxation. After about 5 days they let us all go home for a thirty-day leave.

It was so good to see the folks again. As I walked through my parents' front door, I immediately saw the toll that my six months in combat had taken on my mom. When I stopped home on my way to MacDill Air Force Base back in the fall of 1943, my mom had brown hair. Now it was mostly white. Mom and Dad had been so fearful of losing me over there that they would wait for the mailman each day, hoping for a letter even though they knew that any update that I might send them would be a week or two old. Later, they told me that getting the "Missing in Action" telegram from the War Department when I was shot down on the Merseburg mission, and then not knowing for over a week whether I had survived or not, was one of the worst weeks of their lives.

Mom was a bit shocked that I had lost quite a bit of weight, but mostly I remember it as "there's no place like home." Brother Joe was also there, but we really didn't pal around much as he had his usual busy girlfriend schedule. My high school tennis buddy, Gene Fears, was home from the merchant marine, so we had a good time. Gene had been around the world four or five times, and I enjoyed hearing about his adventures.

One sad note is that I learned that Grandpa died in his sleep while I was crossing the Atlantic in April. I think that he was 86 but had no apparent illness. I had really been looking forward to seeing him again . . . I don't think I mentioned this before (in my journal), but Grandpa Hahn was originally from Munich, Germany. He came over to the States as a young man in 1880 or so and became a successful jeweler. I grew up in a large three-story house and my grandparents lived with us, so we were all very close. I went on two bombing missions to Munich, and by war's end there wasn't much left of his birthplace. War is a terrible business . . . but I had no intention of sharing that or any of my combat experiences with my family.

Back at Santa Anna, aerial gunners were being assigned to B-29 heavy bombers for the war in the Pacific. I'll never forget this big army colonel who gave me my AF 64 physical. He looked at me and my records and said something to the effect of "How did you fly thirty-five missions over Europe when you are colorblind, cross-eyed, and some twenty pounds underweight?" Then he kind of laughed and said he understood that being a gunner, you didn't need all of those qualifications. He then asked if I wanted to be assigned to B-29s. I guess I chickened out as I said something like, "I've really had enough—if that's okay with you, sir."

He then said I had 140 points, which was enough to retire (you needed 85 points, which was a combination of length of service, age, etc., but I had extra points for overseas duty, combat flights, etc.). He stamped my papers and then turned them around so that I could see it: "GROUNDED!"

So that meant that my flying days were over—what a feeling!

Then they sent me to Rantoul, Illinois—the Chanute Air Force Base for discharge—or reassignment to some ground duty. While I was there, they asked me if I wanted to sign up for the regular Army as a career. As I recall, that didn't interest me although I didn't have any idea what I would do when I became a civilian.

The CO assigned me to the orderly room, where I mainly did secretarial type of work. But the point system came into play and really helped in moving me up the list of prospective discharge candidates. As I think I mentioned, I had a bunch; although I had only been in service about twenty months, the combat duty and medals really added points to the amount of service and your age requirements.

Rantoul was only about 150 miles from St. Louis, so I had fun coming home on most weekends. I'd take a Greyhound bus, and I'll never forget some of those wild rides. It was at night and the drivers would go 70 or 80 mph on the narrow, curvy, two-lane highways, so it was impossible to sleep. These drivers would speed along so that they could have a cup of coffee with their buddies at the many stops.

As I remember, I stayed at Chanute for about four months and was discharged about October 1, 1945. It seems like those four months took forever to pass by, but eventually I was done.

So, I could say that this is where my tale comes to its end . . . but it is also the perfect place to tell a final story about my time at Ridgewell, something that happened that always stuck with me, kind of a sweet thing. But it also sums up how tenuous our existence was over there in combat.

When I got my orders to return to the States, the word must have gotten around. There was a cook that was famous for being the biggest grouch on the base. He seemed to hate his job, and I knew he didn't like me. I could mention the World Series, or the weather, and he would just scowl and turn away. Anyway, he must have heard I had my orders (to leave the base), and after I went through the chow line he came over to our table at lunch, chatting, all friendly-like, and asked me to stop by the back-kitchen receiving door. I had been there over eight months, and this was the first time I got a civil word from him. I didn't know what to think . . .

When I did go to the back door, bless his heart, he gave me a gift of oranges, apples, and a grapefruit. An armload of fresh fruit! And congratulated me. I was overwhelmed. So he did have some feelings for us—although he surely didn't show them. I think he had been there from the start and no doubt had gotten tired of getting to know the crews, guys like me, and then hearing about them getting killed or taken POW. So he put up his walls like so many of us had to do, and just stopped making new friends. Self-preservation, I guess. But when he knew I was out of harm's way, he gave me that little gift, and I will never forget his kind gesture.

CHAPTER 17
WAR AND REMEMBRANCE

Mission 36: November 1945 St. Louis, Missouri to enjoy civilian life again

Bob Harper:

Like a lot of men returning from the war, I needed some time to adjust to civilian life. And adjust to the peace and quiet and all the things that we take for granted. Though I would joke with my dad about being a drain on the family resources, I still had some money set aside. So, I thought I would just connect with my friends and family again and take it easy. But after only about ten days at home, I was bored, probably restless is a better word for it, and decided to go to an employment agency (Kay Williams). They sent me to three St. Louis companies. I think it was Westinghouse, St. Louis Union Trust, and the John Nooter Boiler Works Company.

After going to the first two interviews, it was about two o'clock in the afternoon and I debated if I should go to Nooter, as I didn't have a car and it was in one of St. Louis's dodgy neighborhoods. But I wanted to keep in good with the agency, so I took the Broadway streetcar to 1400 South Broadway and walked through some railroad yards to Nooter's office on Second Street.

I told the receptionist that Kay Williams Agency sent me over, so she gave me a simple one-page application form. I filled it out and checked a box at the bottom that asked if you could type. I was then sent to an office where an older man was smoking a cigar, and he read my form and said, "Son, I see you just got out of the service, but you really can't do very much, can you?"

"No, sir, my education was interrupted," I replied.

Then, looking at my application again, he jabbed a finger at the bottom of the page and asked, "But says here, you can type?"

"I think so; I took typing in high school and did a little in the Army when I got transferred back to the States."

"Well," he said, "we need someone to type payroll checks, so take your coat off and go over and see that tall guy in the next office and help him fill out those payroll checks."

With no intention of taking the job, I told him, "Well, sir, I have several other places to go."

He got up, suddenly looking angry, and waved towards that nearby office, and said, "Son, don't argue with me!" I could tell he meant it. He towered above me, a big Irishman, and scared me to death.

So, I stumbled over to the next office, where a jackhammer was breaking up some concrete so that they could remove a huge 8-foot-tall safe. To make a long story short, I spent the next eighteen months in that payroll department.

Then one day I was talking to a coworker, complaining that my job was going nowhere, and I was going to have to leave Nooter and find something else. That is when I got my second big break. The other clerk mentioned that there was a job opening in Nooter's fledgling sales department. I got the job, and that is where I discovered my passion, sales and photography.

For over four decades I worked at Nooter, a wonderful, employee-owned company. Along the way I finally attended night school at Washington University for six years while holding down my day job. The professors at that prestigious night school were often already involved in the business world and they taught us from real world examples, a little like learning from an experienced gunner compared to just reading about air combat in books. I credit them for some of my success back at Nooter where the company was growing by leaps and bounds. Eventually, I became the vice president of administration and the only non-engineer on Nooter's board of directors, running the workers' pension fund along with other HR responsibilities. Everyone at Nooter knew and trusted me; I had spent my first two years there handing them their paychecks each week!

So, it was a successful, happy life for me, living with my lovely wife, Katy, raising our two children, Jim and Julie. Playing golf again and tennis, just enjoying my hometown of St. Louis. I loved my job at Nooter, eventually running their human resources department and helping that wonderful company grow. I was a busy man, which was a good thing, and it was quite some time before I thought about the war and my days with the 381st at Ridgewell. I stayed in touch with some of my crewmates, Joe Pearce and Gene Weisser, but it wasn't a steady thing, Christmas cards and letters, but we were all pretty busy with our families and careers, and we weren't living close together.

Bob's friend Joe Pearce, the former B-17 pilot, wrote him a letter in 1976. One of the planes that Bob's crew trained on at MacDill AF Base in Florida was the famous "Memphis Belle," one of the first of the 8th Army Air Force B-17s to complete its required twenty-five combat missions. That accomplishment was achieved back in 1942–43, during some of the highest B-17 losses and when very few crews were making it alive through their required twenty-five missions. Thus, the "Memphis Belle" became a symbol of hope for the American bomber crews in England and, just as importantly, for their families as well. When the "Memphis Belle" returned to the States, they flew her from city to city on a big war bond drive. When the fundraising was finally over, the "Memphis Belle" became a training plane at MacDill field. Harper:

> I never paid much attention to the names of the planes that we were flying during training, and even during my time in combat, but after the war was over, our pilot Joe Pearce sent me a letter telling me that he had seen the movie *Memphis Belle* and got quite a kick out of it. We had flown the *Belle* on a couple of training missions in Florida, and he was just tickled to see the movie. I had to laugh; it was news to me.

Bob would continue to hear from his friend Joe Pearce, who became the postmaster of Milford, Delaware. In 1979, Joe began a movement to create a US commemorative postal stamp that would honor the B-17 bomber. Uniquely positioned within the US Post Office, Joe managed to get US postmaster general Bennet on board, along with various congressmen, as well as noted senator and former World War II pilot Barry Goldwater. Joe had also become involved with the group that was restoring the B-17 "Shoo Shoo Baby."

During the war, the 381st's B-17 "Shoo Shoo Baby" was crippled during a bombing mission to Germany but managed to successfully land in Sweden, where her crew was interned. The plane was eventually repaired and used commercially for years until it was disassembled in France and, in 1972, flown in cargo planes to the US Air Force Museum at Wright-Patterson AFB, Ohio. In 1978, it was shipped once more to Dover AFB in Delaware, where, with the help of the 512th Airlift Wing, it was painstakingly restored (a ten-year process that was still underway while Joe campaigned for the stamp).

In his letters to various influencers, Joe expressed the hope that they would use the "Shoo Shoo Baby's" image on a stamp to honor the B-17 and the thousands of men who flew aboard them. He would end each letter with this statement: "Is there anyone in your group who would like to see the Fortress so commemorated? It is hard to believe the once-mighty B-17 is now a War Relic!"

Despite Joe's efforts and inside connections, the B-17 stamp was never issued. But on June 19, 1987, it was announced that a commemorative sheet of stamps featuring World War II Air Force planes would be issued, including one of a B-17 Flying Fortress. The B-17 featured on the stamp had an L in a triangle, the symbol of the 381st Bomb Group, and the number 337675, which was the B-17 known as "Patches" / "Flak Magnet." The bomber was chosen because of an excellent photo taken by a *Times* photographer on August 5, 1944. The photo was studied and then painted by aviation artist Bill Phillips from Oregon. With thousands of B-17s from many bomb groups to choose from, it was quite a coincidence that though almost two decades had passed since pilot Joe Pearce began his campaign for a B-17 stamp, by a twist of fate they chose to use one from Joe's outfit, the 381st BG.

Just four months later, on October 23, 1987, 1Lt. Joseph Pearce, Bob's friend and trusted pilot, passed away, knowing that a final mission had been accomplished.

• • •

A FINAL REMEMBRANCE

In one of our early conversations, Bob told me that at first, he had no interest at all in thinking or talking much about his wartime experiences. However, after a period of decades had passed by, he began to let his mind return to those events, slowly gaining some perspective on what he had gone through:

> A few years after Joe Pearce's passing, Katy and I took a trip to Europe, with a layover in London. We grabbed a cab and took it all the way to the base at Ridgewell, 90 miles or so, stopping in nearby Great Yeldham for lunch. When we told the waitress at the restaurant that I had been stationed with 381st BG during the war, the whole staff really fussed over us, made us feel so welcome!
>
> After lunch we headed over to the old airfield but only spent a short time there because there wasn't much left to see (a wonderful 381st BG Museum now exists on the site). Still, I could make out the old runways where our Fortresses had formed in long lines,

slowly taxiing for takeoff in those early morning hours. The distinct pattern of the runways as seen from above was etched in my mind. They were a symbol that we had made it home to safety, and just needed to get our bomber back down on the ground.

We walked out there onto one of the runways and I closed my eyes. I could hear those big Wright Cyclone engines roaring and to tell the truth, I experienced that uneasy feeling again. That feeling we got when we were getting set for takeoff, not knowing what the day might bring us... To stand out there in the silence, the peaceful silence. You couldn't help but feel for all the boys that never made it back. It was a very emotional moment or two, as you might expect.

Back in the States, I joined the St. Louis Chapter of the 8th Air Force Memorial Group where I got to know some of the men of the other Bomb Groups that were living in our area. We didn't talk much about the war at our get-togethers, we talked more about our families and our jobs and spent some quality time together on the golf courses. Having been through that war and experienced roughly the same things, for the most part there was just no need to revisit it at all. It was a quiet sort of bond but a very strong one.

Over the years I slowly began reading books about World War II, one aspect of it or another. Churchill, Roosevelt, Eisenhower, Patton, et al. and the complicated campaigns, along with the Allied strategy in the Far East as well as in Europe. I started to learn more about the bigger picture and the tough decisions that were made, much of which was suppressed for years, and certainly not available to us while I was in the service. Of course, we knew back then that the Germans, the Nazis, were doing some horrible things, but it was only later on that I learned more about what was happening in the territories that they had conquered, and more about their treatments of prisoners of war and of their atrocities in the death camps. . . . And most importantly, their plans to take their evil way of life out into the world, and the secret weapons that, given the chance, might have allowed them to be successful.

I also slowly came to grips with my role in the 8th Air Force, reading some wonderful books along the way by others who had seen combat like me, and who just didn't want to think about it . . . until they finally did. And of course, if anyone wants to get a glimpse of what we went through, I still highly recommend the movie *Twelve O' Clock High*, with Gregory Peck. I don't think anyone ever told the story as well as that one does. And for a big look at the 8th Air Force, I have to say, *Masters of the Air* really is my favorite book.

I eventually came around a bit in my way of viewing those months of combat: I would never wish my experiences on a single soul, not what I witnessed and went through firsthand. But I am glad that I helped out, and glad that I did my very small part in that very big war. Which reminds me, I also have one last little story for you, my last brush with the enemy. Strangely enough, this took place decades after the war was over.

My wife and I decided as we grew older that we no longer needed to be in our big home in St. Louis, and we found a lovely retirement community to move to. It had all the bells and whistles, and we were blessed to be able to live out our lives in comfort there, among our peer group, with lots of opportunities to stay healthy and active and to meet new people.

It was the type of place where conversations flowed freely, and if you were shy, that was quickly overcome by the friendly staff and other residents. One day Katy and I were sitting in the dining room, just finishing up one of those lovely desserts, and I noticed a new couple at the table next to ours. So as was the custom, to make them feel welcome, I leaned over and introduced Katy and myself. Their names were Willie and Christel, and though our first conversation was brief, I noticed that Willie had a very strong German accent.

A couple of days later, I saw Willie sitting alone in one of the lounges, having a coffee, and went over and joined him. It wasn't long before I asked him, "So where were you during the war?"

When he answered, you could have knocked me over with a feather. "I was with the 14th Flak Division, stationed at a little city called Merseburg . . . you know of it?"

"I surely do," I answered. "I was with the 381st Bomb Group out of England . . . B-17 Flying Fortresses. Do you remember if you were at Merseburg in November of 1944?" I asked.

Willie hesitated for a moment. Now it was his turn to look a little uncomfortable . . . "Yes, we were there, I was there for sure . . ."

"Do you think you might have been there on November 21st? I was shot down that day."

He hesitated again but then answered me honestly. "Yes, I am sure that I was there. We never got a day off, and if you came to bomb us then I would have been there . . . shooting at you . . ."

We both laughed. My plane had lost two engines to flak that day. I gave him the story, very briefly. He said that he was glad that I made it back, that I had managed to parachute to safety and wasn't injured. Of course, I told him the same thing; that I was happy he had survived the war.

I had no hard feelings, of course, and I don't think he did either, but after that conversation, it remained kind of formal between us. Friendly, but formal. We would say hello and chat a little, Willie was a nice guy, and his wife, Christel, was a lovely, lovely lady who became a good friend of my wife, Katy. I called Willie, Sharpshooter, and maybe it was just out of habit, but I found myself keeping an eye on him . . . I guess old habits die hard . . .

Then Bob laughed, and so did I.

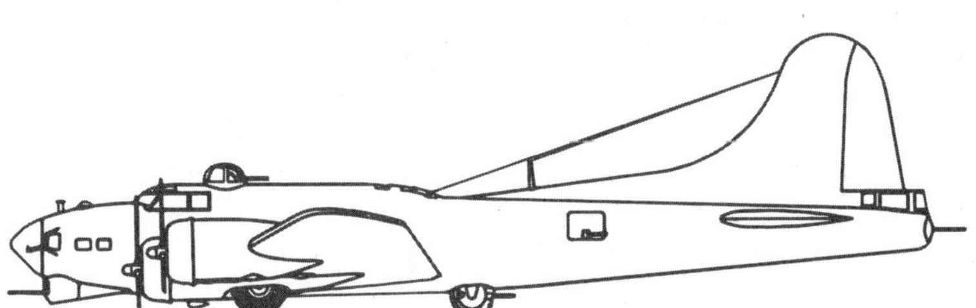

EPILOGUE

During the six years that it took to research Bob's story, which included time off to work on some fiction projects and to read at length the thirty or forty books and articles that would equip me with the necessary background to put this story into the context of the greater war, I also had the distinct pleasure of really getting to know Bob Harper.

More than once, Bob remarked humbly, "Well, if you think anyone would be interested in reading it, I am glad to share my thoughts and memories of that time." And though I wish that I could have done some of the interviewing earlier in Bob's retirement years, it was an amazing experience to work with a person in his nineties who was "still sharp as a tack" (one of Bob's expressions).

In 2018, I managed to interview Robert Pearce, the nephew of pilot Joe Pearce, who generously shared his own research with me about his uncle's time in the service, including a letter from the 381st's own chaplain, James Brown. Thirty years after the war ended, Joe Pearce had managed to locate Chaplain Brown and sent him a letter, hoping to connect with him again. Chaplain Brown had counseled the men of the 381st BG from the group's formation in Pyote, Texas, to its final days in Ridgewell, England. Chaplain Brown not only provided a friendly ear and support for hundreds of airmen who feared that they wouldn't make it through their missions alive, but he also managed to go along on five combat missions with them. Chaplain Brown later wrote a great book about these experiences, titled *The Men of the Mighty 381st.* Unfortunately this limited-edition volume is now out of print.

I think the perfect way to end Bob's story is to share the letter that Father Brown wrote back to pilot Joe Pearce.

December 19, 1977

Colonel James G Brown, Chaplain 381st Bomb Group
Haverhill, New Hampshire, 03765
Hi, Joseph J. Pearce Jr.
Pilot of the 381st Bombardment Group

To you who piloted our B-17s—Flying Fortresses—on Ridgewell Air Drome, England, you who were among the greatest and finest group of men I have ever known. As a clergyman I have met men of all ranks and stages of life, and men in every category of business and professions, yet I have never seen a body of men with such great character and sense of responsibility as the pilots of my bomb group. I shall forever stand in awe of them. Thus, I here and now pay my highest respect to you, and to all the men who served with me in the 381st Bomb Group.

I would like to say also that my admiration goes to the navigators, bombardiers, radiomen, engineers, and gunners who climbed into those Flying Fortresses and headed into the unknown. I sat with them night after night, and every night for more than two years. They were a great body of men. I cannot speak for the other bomb groups, but I can speak for the 381st, of which I was chaplain from its formation in Pyote, Texas, until it was disbanded in Sioux Falls, South Dakota, after the war. I was the first and only bomb group chaplain of the 381st. There was another chaplain on the Base, but he was not the 381st chaplain. He did not go overseas with us and was not at Ridgewell Air Drome at first. He was sent on as an "overage" (if that be the word) and was an extra to meet the needs of the Roman Catholic men of the base. What I am saying is: A bomb group called for only one chaplain. I am very grateful to have had that honor.

Well: you have the right man. I AM your chaplain. And you have brought to me a great deal of happiness by your letter. Was I surprised!? Indeed, I was. My wife Valerie and I read the letter as we stood outside the post office, and she beamed all over. She knows how highly I think of my men of the 381st.

You surely pinpoint me because of my 90-mile ride in one day to London to preach in a church. I bicycled both ways in one day, beginning at 12:00 noon after I conducted the morning services in the chapel. I rushed to the mess hall (actually the kitchen) and there picked up a chicken drumstick which I ate on the way, steering the bicycle with one hand.

Where I got caught was this: when I promised the London minister to preach in his church, I thought I could get a train from Ridgewell to London on Sunday. To my amazement I learned that there were no trains in that small line on Sunday. I then asked the motor pool for transportation by Jeep. They of course said, "Yes," because they were always good to me. But on that Sunday, we were flying in combat. All the Jeeps were busy. So, I said to myself: nothing would stop me from keeping my engagement, in the London pulpit. I'll make it if I have to bicycle all the way, and this I did, getting there for the 6:30 service.

But this fact you may not know. When he met me at the church at 6:00 p.m., he said, "I cannot take you to tea in the vicarage (the parsonage) because it has been bombed out and completely destroyed during the past week." He only smiled and responded further, "What a nuisance those doodle bombs!"—meaning the V-1 rockets. He didn't seem at all disturbed by it. Calm like all Englishmen. I then pedaled the bicycle slowly as he walked beside me, to have tea at the home of a deacon just a block from the church. We were back to the church for the 6:30 evening service.

Then—I bicycled back to the base that night from London—all the way in a tight fog, so thick you could cut it with a knife and eat it with a spoon. I bicycled onto the base, through the gates, about 4:00 a.m. The MPs at the gate could not believe their eyes when they saw me, at that time of the morning, and absolutely soaking wet from the dense fog. But I was satisfied. I had fulfilled my appointment.

You are right on count No. 2. (But I am surprised that you remember all these things.) Yes, I am the chaplain who went on a bombing mission. As you say, to get the feel of it.

I was telling my men day after day that they had to go. There was no way out unless they were sick. But I felt like a fool telling them that when I sat back in England in an easy chair. Perhaps I should say, a safe chair. This I could not do, so, from the very first, I begged our commanding officer, Joe Nazzaro, to allow me to go. He was a great man, and a strict officer, so he said flatly, "You are not allowed in combat." One does not argue with a man like that. And, of course, I would not violate his command.

I therefore did not fly in combat as a stowaway. [*Author's note*: I believe that in Joe Pearce's letter to Chaplain Brown, he refers to Brown slipping aboard combat missions as being a stowaway.] This I would not do. I would only go with the full permission of my commanding officer.

When Col. Nazzaro left the 381st, a new colonel came to the Base as commanding officer. His name was LEBER. One of my first words to him were "I want to fly in combat." He replied, "You don't want to fly in combat; you'll get shot down."

That was the wrong answer, and I knew it. I therefore kept after him until one night in briefing he came over to me and said: "This is your mission. We are going to Frankfurt." I was ready for combat, as I had been night after night—dressed in flying clothes—heavy fleece-lined jacket and long fleece-lined pants and helmet; also, my parachute which I had gotten when we trained at Pyote Air Base. I had it with me each night at briefing so that I would be ready when Col. Leber said, "Go."

How pleased all the men were. And I was thrilled. Off we went into the wild blue yonder. But it wasn't all that simple, as you well know. Frankfurt was well fortified with ground guns, as you well know. And the German fighters were at us by the hundreds, as you well know. I was in the lead plane and saw some of my men go down in flames next to me. It was rough. But I was glad I was there with the men and not back in England. Our plane made it back. [Chaplain Brown would fly with the men on five combat missions.]

Later I was all dressed for combat and was about to go on the very first raid over Berlin. I was to fly with MILLER, who was in the lead plane. I should have left the briefing room early and gone to his plane. As I sat with Miller and his crew at briefing, Col. LEBER saw me in flying clothes. He said, "Where are you going, chaplain?" I replied, "I'm going to Berlin." He replied, "Like Hell you are; I got hell from the commanding general for allowing you to go on other raids."

Word had gotten around the air bases that Chaplain Brown had gone on combat raids. The general therefore had reprimanded Colonel LEBER for allowing me to go.

All this means that I really was not a stowaway but sat with my men in the briefing room and was given permission by the commanding officer to fly in combat. Naturally therefore, Col. LEBER was not angry with me.

However, that ended my going on bombing raids. But it was worth it, because for months afterwards, when new fliers came onto the Base, they said, "Hey, you are the chaplain who flew in combat with your men."

Well, pilot Pearce, you wrote to the right Chaplain Brown, and I am delighted. I hope that someday I can drop in to visit you when I pass through Delaware.

After coming back from England with the bomb group when the war was over (we stayed until the very end), the bomb group landed in Sioux Falls, South Dakota. We were headed for Japan. But dropping the atomic bomb brought an end to the war. Notwithstanding, the Air Force kept me in for another year, even though I had the points to get out.

I returned to my civilian parish and have just retired from my church one year ago. I moved from my Connecticut church to a little town in New Hampshire. Here it is quiet and peaceful, and I love it very much.

I remained in the Air Force for 23 years in the Reserve. I just retired a few years ago. Thus, I remained close to the Air Force all these years. Never will I forget my days with my men of the 381st Bombardment Group. They were an inspiration to me, and a great group of men.

Thanks for writing to me. Have a Merry Christmas,

Cheerio,
Chaplain Brown

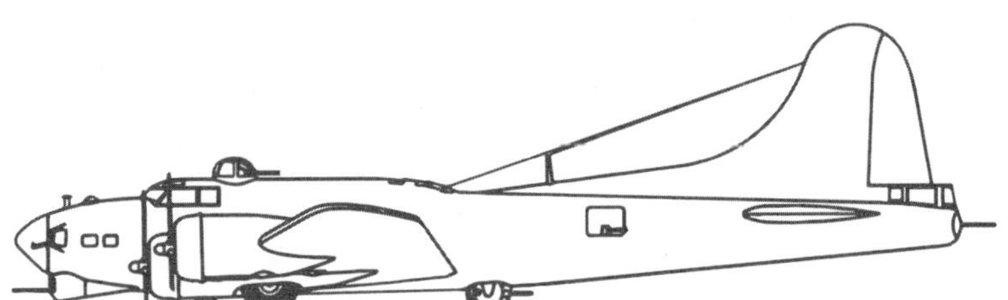

AUTHOR'S INVITATION, APRIL 2023

At one hundred years old, Bob Harper is now the last living member of his combat crew. We hope that you, our readers, will see this book as a salute to those men whom Bob served with, and a tribute to the many, many other brave young airmen who never got to tell their own stories. We also hope that if we have done a good job here, you will share the book with your friends and families.

Bob Harper in 2019:

> I only did my very small part, Bill. We all felt that we were lucky when it was all said and done, and that it was a miracle that we came through it. The weather. The flak. The enemy, the German fighter pilots, who were quite good at what they did. And the B-17 flying 5 miles above the earth, wingtip to wingtip, a necessary invitation to collision and disaster. Despite what felt like terrible odds, each morning when we climbed into that B-17 together, we were a team, supporting each other the best we could . . . I hope that in a small way, my crew and the many men of the 381st BG helped make a difference in ending that terrible war.

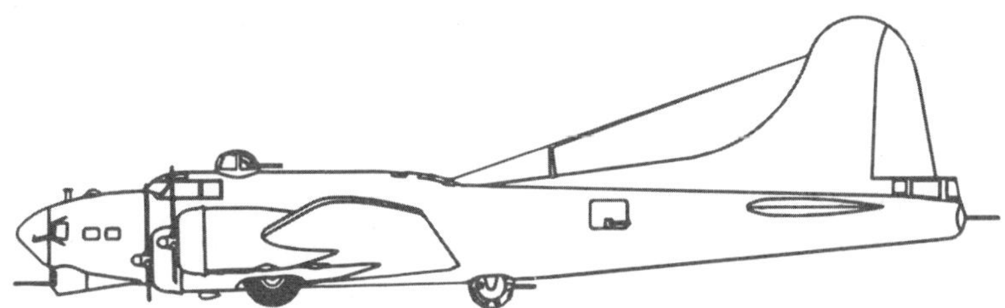

BIBLIOGRAPHY

Articles

Blanchard, Robert. "Sobering Stats: 15,000 U.S. Airmen Killed in Training in WW II." RealClearHistory, February 12, 2019.

Dunlap, David W. "Ex-Gunner Spots a Model of His B-17, Downed in '44." *New York Times*, August 15, 1982.

Grant, Rebecca. "Twenty Missions in Hell." *Air and Space Forces Magazine*, April 1, 2007.

"Mechanical Brains: Working in Metal Boxes, Computing Devices Aim Guns and Bombs with Inhuman Accuracy." *Life*, January 24, 1944.

Vento, Carol Schultz. "Treatment of War[-]Related Psychiatric Injuries Post–World War II." Defense Media Network, February 12, 2012.

Books

Bingley, Paul, and Mike Peters. *Bomb Group: The 8th Air Force's 381st and the Allied Air Offensive over Europe*. Havertown, PA: Casemate, 2022.

Carr, Edward C. *On Final Approach*. Coupeville, WA: Edward C. Carr, 2002.

Craven, Wesley Frank, and James Lea Cate, eds. *The Army Air Forces in World War II*. Vol. 3, *Europe: Argument to V-E Day, January 1944 to May 1945*. Washington, DC: Office of Air Force History, 1984.

Farr, Frank. *Flak Happy*. Bloomington, IN: AuthorHouse, 2011.

Gaillard, Ernest, Jr. (lieutenant colonel, MD USAAF-MC, ret.). *Flight Surgeon*. Bloomington, IN: 1stBooks, 2005.

Jones, Troy H., Jr. *Some Recollections of a Florida Cracker*. Unpublished memoir, 1992.

Mackay, Ron. *Ridgewell's Flying Fortresses: The 381st Bombardment Group (H) in World War II*. Atglen, PA: Schiffer Military History, 2000.

Maurer, Kevin. *Damn Lucky: One Man's Courage during the Bloodiest Military Campaign in Aviation History*. New York: St. Martins, 2022.

Miller, Donald. *Masters of the Air: America's Bomber Boys Who Fought the Air War against Nazi Germany*. New York: Simon & Schuster, 2007.

Stiles, Bert. *Serenade to the Big Bird: A True Account of Life and Death from Inside the Cockpit*. Washington, DC: Pickles Partners, 2013.

Journals and manuals

The 381st Bomb Group War Diary (1943–1945), USAF Records, by 1Lt. Saul B. Schwartz, AC, group historian.

The 533rd Bomb Squadron War Diary (1943–1945), USAF Records, Transcribed from microfilm by Dave Osborne.

Hansell, Haywood S., Jr. (USAF major general, ret.). *The Strategic Air War against Germany and Japan: A Memoir*. USAF Warrior Studies, Office of USAF History, 1986.

Psychiatric Experiences of the Eighth Air Force: First Year of Combat (July 4, 1942–July 4, 1943). US Air Force.

This Is Your Gun. Army Air Force Manual, 1943.

The United States Strategic Bombing Surveys. Maxwell Air Force Base, AL: Alabama Air University Press, October 1987.